MARSHALL GOINS

FUTURE FREEDOM

The Reason
Why You
Must Have
**a Financial
Plan**

Future Freedom

The Reason Why You Must Have A Retirement Plan

By

Marshall Goins

Print in the United States of America.

First edition: January 2017

ISBN: 978-1-365-71363-7

This book is dedicated to
my family and friends
who will benefit from this advice.

CONTENTS

PREFACE:

What If There Was a Family Friend That Could Help You, And You Didn't Know It?

From time to time I hear about a financial disaster. Not the global kind of financial disaster we hear about every couple years. The personal financial disaster that can happen because people just don't know.

Of course some financial disasters are just bad luck. Sometimes bad things happen and we have to dig ourselves out. The personal financial disaster I'm speaking of can be avoided.

If you are not in the financial services business, it may be hard to realize how badly people can mess up their lives by making decisions without seeking advice. Sometimes we just don't know what we don't know.

As a person that advises others for a living, at times I think about all the people I know, family and friends. Some of them know what I do, some of them don't. Some of them have heard what I do but have forgotten. This happens to me all the time. I forget a lot of stuff and so do you.

This book is written for my family, friends, and prospective clients. It is my hope that maybe, just maybe, you will come to a point in your life when you need advice. It is my hope that you may remember me and seek my council.

This book is a compilation of ideas and concepts that I have collected over the years. When I have face to face meetings with a client or a friend, many of these ideas come up in conversation. You never really know how much people remember about a conversation, but this book is a reference point. What would Marshall say about term life insurance, or annuities, or saving money? This book is a reflection of this thinking.

Over the years, I have been privileged to work in the area of financial services. In this time, I have seen a lot of different financial circumstances.

As an advisor, I see the messes and mistakes that people make with their financial lives. This book is written in the hope that maybe I can help you avoid one of these messes.

Many people don't know what they don't know about their finances. No area is more apt to this comment than finances. Whether we are talking about investments or taxes or whatever, there are lots of smart people doing lots of smart things. How much time have you spent studying what they have learned?

Studies show that people who are educated about their finances and play a role in planning their financial future will be twice as rich as those who haven't a clue. Most Americans have not planned for retirement. I don't want you to be one of those people.

Financial literacy is surprisingly low. Retirement planning is a strong predictor of retirement wealth. If you learn how much you will need at retirement, you are much more likely to achieve your goals. These are simple ideas but are you taking action? Have you called someone that can help? Have you attended the class or watched the video online? If not then, why not?

Why are some people and families more motivated, more focused, and more wealthy than others? Why do some people take action and other don't? Why do some people seek help and others don't? It all starts with "why". What is your purpose, your reason, your why?

In this book, I hope to give you a kick start in the direction of your why. I believe, I believe, I believe, that if you focus on freedom and what you enjoy, your motivation will increase. If you can imagine, just for a minute, what freedom feels like you will do what I am recommending in this book.

Future freedom is what we all want. And a financial plan is the first step to becoming financially free. You can wait for luck to find you. Or, you can increase the chances that luck will find you. A financial plan is the first step.

We start with why because creating a financial plan is not very exciting. It is only one-step in a process. The idea of retirement is not very exciting. But many people claim that retirement is their number one goal in life.

The thing that excites me is freedom. America was created on this idea. I believe that the reason and the purpose for financial success and wealth is freedom. Freedom of time, freedom to spend time as you chose. Freedom to spend time with people you like. Freedom to work on the projects you enjoy. That is motivating. That is a step towards your why.

But you have a part to play. You have to fill in the blanks. I want to be free because then I can _____. I want to be financially free so that I can _____. I want to be free to spend time with _____. I want to be free to give my time, attention and treasure to _____.

You have to fill in the blanks. The blank is where the real juice is found. The blank is where the core motivation resides and it all becomes very personal and powerful. This book is driven by a cause, by a purpose, by a belief. And that is to get you moving in the direction of freedom.

Many people never determine what their why is. They are too busy with what they have to do to make a living. They are too busy with how they are going to pay the bills. Getting to what will inspire you to seek freedom is hard. But that is where all the good stuff lives.

If my life and my experience can help you, so be it. I firmly believe that happiness is a possibility. I firmly believe that freedom is a possibility. I may be further along the path of freedom than you are, let me help you. You may be further along the path than I am, call me and help me.

Sincerely,

Marshall Goins
December 31, 2016

"An investment in knowledge pays the best interest." - Benjamin Franklin

Introduction

If you are just starting your journey on the financial road to success, this book is for you. If you've been on the road a while, you may see some useful road signs to alter your direction. If you wonder what you've been doing wrong and why you're not as financially successful as you'd like to be, I suspect you will find some novel ideas here.

This book is titled Future Freedom because I believe freedom is what we all crave. At many levels we want freedom to speak our minds, freedom to spend our time as we choose, freedom to spend time with people we enjoy.

This book is focused on financial freedom because many of the other freedoms are based on the ability to get your financial house in order. Financial freedom is a power step in getting your freedom in other areas. Once financial "success" is achieved you are free to spend your time as you see fit.

For many of us, that financial freedom does not come until you retire. As you may realize this book is about the topic of retirement but we will not be using the word retirement. I don't like the word. The word implies, and literally means, "to be put out to pasture", past your prime, not useful any longer. Retirement is not very exciting. I have hundreds of clients and the most happy and energetic clients are not really retired. They are working on projects that they enjoy. Their financial success has enabled them the freedom to choose how they will spend their time.

This can be your story and you don't have to wait until retirement.

Freedom is much more exciting and motivating. And I believe the understanding of what financial freedom can mean to you and your family will help you get motivated as well.

While this book is about financial freedom, freedom in other dimensions of life is a key element to a happy life. Consider physical freedom. We all know the stories of slaves and the happiness of their release. Whether it is the children of Israel and their release from Egypt or the American slaves of the 19th century, physical freedom is something we would all fight for. Are you willing to fight for your financial freedom?

Consider freedom of expression.

Consider religious freedom.

FREEDOM

Of course, freedom without proper restraint can create its own set of problems. Maybe the combination of what you know and what I share in this book will be just what you need to get over the hump.

Many people may believe that financial success is an accident, or that success is based on your innate talent. Maybe luck had something to do with it. Who knows! Maybe it is a balance of all of this. I suspect it is a combination of factors.

All I know for sure is that the financially successful have created a system and a roadmap to their destination. Yes, some have gotten lucky but as you will recognize if you've ever studied the lives of lottery winners, it's not about the money. It's about the character of the hand holding the purse strings. The story of lottery winners is, in most cases, a tragic tale.

As Jim Rohn is famous for saying,

"it's not about the money, it's about the person you become to achieve it."

This means that if you lost a million dollars, you could earn it all back because the wealth is about the person you have become.

Talent, luck, or hard work, maybe it is a combination of all three. But, I do know that your chances are better if you plan, make the effort, and develop a conscious strategy of managing opportunities. If you pick up some ideas in this book and go on to great financial success, you might think you know how you did it.

The reason will probably have something to do with the many levels of your personal awesomeness. And that will be fine. That's just how human brains work. It is hard to determine the real reason for our success.

In this book, we will observe many of the ways the human brain works, and how it can help us and deceives us. This process of thinking and doing is critical to your financial success. It is critical to your ability to save money, create a budget, pick advisors to help you.

The only reason you may not have all these things in place now is because of the ideas you are holding in your head. Some of these may be helping you, and some are definitely not helping.

My hope is that this book will help bring clarity to your thinking about your financial life.

We all know money distorts truth. It is hard to know what to do when it comes to money. Especially when you consider the relationships, the implications, the feelings. It can get very complicated. When it comes to financial issues and financial planning, one size does not fit all.

My hope for this book is that it will initiate a process of discovery, drive your curiosity, and goose your interest in the areas of money. As we have said, your mind is the most important element in successful saving and investing.

It has been said that …happiness is health plus freedom

HEALTH + FREEDOM = HAPPINESS

GOOD HEALTH plus FINANCIAL FREEDOM equals HAPPINESS

PHYSICAL HEALTH + FREEDOM TO SET MY OWN SCHEDULE = HAPPINESS

In my experience, this is pretty close to true. If you believe differently, that's okay too. Everything in this book is accurate, as far as I know. I really don't have all the answers. That's why I try to stay connected with other smart people, other investment professionals, tax professionals, legal professionals, relationship experts. It all helps.

Before you decide if this book is rubbish, give some of it a try. I don't have the corner on truth. When it comes to complicated questions like financial planning, humility is the only sensible point of view. I do my best to direct people in wise financial decisions. I study and prepare and do my best.

Most people spend very little time thinking about the important issues of life. I can't say that I'm much different, but I have spent a lot of time thinking about how to help people make better financial decisions.

Most people have poor filters when it comes to knowing the truth about how to manage their money. That why it helps to have a smart friend.

Unfortunately, not everyone has a smart friend. If you are one of the blessed, a smart friend can save you a lot of time and effort. If you do not have smart friend, I hear by appoint myself your smart friend. At least when it comes to financial matters.

Many of these topics make for awkward dinner conversation. Most people get uncomfortable talking about money. As you will hear later, money usually comes with strings attached. Advice about money can have strings as well.

Most of this book is a simplification. Life is really much more complicated. I like to be a simplifier because it makes things more understandable. My best advice is to educate yourself, ask smart friends for help, and seek professional help.

My goal is not to be 100 percent right, my goal is to motivate you to move in the direction that creates freedom for you and your family. Let me know how it turns out.

What is money, really?

Money does not exist. That's right, I said it. Money does not exist in the "real world". In the real world of tangible material objects, money does not exist. I can hear you saying, "What about gold?"

Did you ever consider the fact that outside the mind of the human being money does not exist. No other mammal or other beast has devised a system of money. No other species has devised an abstract system of exchange like money. Yes, some primates may exchange items but no other animal has created a system of money.

This is very good news, money is an idea. Money is something in the mind of man. This is a very interesting thought. Money is a concept humans have created to facilitate our existence.

When you think about all the stress we all have around money, it makes you wonder, where is the stress really coming from. When you think about all the work we humans do for money, you have to wonder, is it really about the money? Maybe it is about something much deeper.

The formal definition of money is something generally accepted as a medium of exchange. It is a measure of value, or a means of payment. Such as an officially coined or stamped metal currency or paper money.

It is amazing how focused we all can be around money. Many of us believe our lives are all about money. In reality and by definition money is just a medium, or method, of exchange.

But what is being exchanged?

Another unique aspect of human beings is our ability to create. Our history is filled with all the wonderful things we have created. From the wheel, to the printing press, to the computer, to the iPhone. We humans have created some amazing things.

Money is just a method of exchanging those things.

Another thing we do as humans is care for others. This is known as service. Money is used as a method to exchange services. You scratch my back and I'll pay you, (or scratch your back).

But, why such a focus on money: the medium of exchange? My contention is that the direct focus on money is not a productive use of time.

Now, you might be saying, but, Marshall, aren't you a financial advisor? Isn't your focus on money? What we do as financial advisors is a service. We serve our clients and share ideas and concepts about protecting and growing their money. We get paid for service, (more on what we do to serve our clients later).

A productive use of time is to focus on creating something of value. That might be a product or a service.

Let's get back to the idea that money is only in your mind. There is a reason why this is so, so important. It is because your wealth, or lack of it, has to do with how you think about money. The way you save money, or don't save money, has to do with how your think about money. The way you invest, has everything to do with how you think.

This book, will hopefully, give you some ideas on how to put money in its proper perspective.

The reason why it is so important to put money in its proper perspective is that if you don't it will literally **kill you**. Yes, that's right. If you don't think about money properly it will kill you. Kind of ridiculous, right?

Consider all the stress some people have around money and possessions. We all know that stress, if it persists over time, will kill you. Consider how angry people get when they don't get the money they feel they deserve. I am sure you all know of examples of people that killed for money.

It is clear to me that money is much more than a medium of exchange. It is an idea in your mind that implies many things. If you don't have enough, it means you're going to starve. If someone takes your money, it means that maybe I should find them and beat them up, (kind of funny but it happens every day as you know).

Money, as they say, has strings attached. The purpose of this book will be to help get the proper strings attached. We want to get the proper strings attached to the way you think about money and saving and investing.

There are so many bad ideas around this topic. That means that I have my work cut out for me.

So, what is money, really? It is a method of exchange that comes with strings attached.

Money & Relationships

Money effects every relationship in our lives. Think about it, parents and children, husbands and wives, employers and employees, friends and acquaintances. Money touches all our relationships in one way or another. The key question is how are we going to set boundaries so that money contributes to great relationships and does not destroy relationships? What are the limits of our giving and receiving? What are our guidelines about money? Who are we comfortable giving money to? Who are we comfortable receiving money from? Who do we owe? Who owes us? What is your expectation as the giver? What are your expectations as the receiver? These are important questions.

It all starts with our personal relationship to money. Understanding what money is and what money is not. We've talked about money being an idea that humans created for a purpose. If we understand the purpose and limitations of money, we can use money for good in our relationships.

We don't always spend a lot of time thinking about these issues but they are real and have an impact each and every day. As a financial advisor, you see it with married couples, you see it with parents and children. Money is the number one reason for marriage failure. It is real and it is important to understand the implications of money on our relationships.

GIVING and RECEIVING
EXPECTIONS: High or Low

Are you still a skeptic about the role of money in our relationships? Just ask yourself this question, do people fight about money? We all know that people fight about money every minute of every day. The question is why, why do we feel the need to fight about money? The core issue is fear. Fear there won't be enough. Fear you won't get your "fair share". Fear that the money will run out and there won't be any more.

How can you get past the fear about money? It is important to realize the money is a tool that we use for exchange. But money is also a concept of the heart and mind. Dealing with the heart and mind is critical to your success in your relationships when it comes to money.

Here are a couple ideas to ponder that may help you reduce the fear.

- Wealth and poverty are in your own mind. You could be rich with ten dollars or poor with a billion dollars. It is just your story about money that strikes fear in your heart.
- Money does not buy happiness. Happiness comes from something else. Happiness comes from a grateful heart. Happiness has nothing to do with money. We all know of the happy poor person and the miserable millionaire. What is going on?
- Money will only make you more of what you already are. If you are a generous person and you inherit a million dollars, you will become more generous. If you have a tendency to drink too much and you inherit a million dollars, you can now become a full time drunk. Sorry but true.

- Financial security is a state of mind. Financial security is not an amount, it is not an account filled to the brim. Security comes from something else. The story we tell ourselves about money is what creates the fear and insecurity. Change the story.
- The truth is, you are supposed to have as much money as you have right now. This is not a theory, this is a fact. It is reality. You're supposed to have more money than you have? I don't think so. You're supposed to have less money? I don't think so. You're supposed to have exactly what you have. If you don't believe it, look at your checkbook.
- If you think money can solve your problems, and you have no money, you will feel helpless to solve your problems. If you think money can solve your problems, and you have lots of money, you will soon realize that you still have problems. Go figure. What is the issue?

Our relationships with people and our relationships with money are intricately connected. Money can destroy relationships faster than any other known material. Why is this true? Because we don't understand the power and the role of money in our lives.

Money creates ties that bind. The definition of a contract is a written or spoken agreement. Money can create unspoken contracts we may not even realize. Even with strangers, it binds us together. It is important to create binds that benefit and not hinder our relationships.

For some of us, our lives are controlled by our thoughts about work and money. The bottom line is, money has an impact on every relationship in our lives. Becoming aware of the impact money can have on relationships is the first step in making our relationships strong and long lasting. It's really not about the money but it can be hard to separate the issues.

Let's get started getting some key ideas about money setup and working for our benefit.

"I will prepare and some day my chance will come."   – Abraham Lincoln

PART 1:
The Preparation

Before we jump into the detail of creating a financial plan, we need to do some basic housekeeping. There are only a few items you need to have in place to start a financial plan. Most people believe you need to wait until you get close to retirement to start. Many people believe that you need to have a nice size nest egg before you start. Many people believe you need to be a certain age to start. None of this is necessary.

There are only three things that you need to get in place before you create a financial plan. This may seem simple but many times simple is the best. The three things are:

1. Find an Income
2. Establish a Budget
3. Setup a System to Save

The first step, find an income, is commonly known as getting a job. The reason we call this, find an income is because there are other ways to generate income other than getting a job. Some people might start a business, some people might join a network marketing company, others might sell things they've made. This can take many forms depending on your stage of life and level of skill.

The second step is also a common step in getting your life on track, establish a monthly budget. This may sound boring but it is vitally important to get a handle on your financial life. If you can't create and maintain a budget it is very hard to set aside money to save and invest. For whatever reason, there is a tendency for most people to spend everything they receive if they don't setup boundaries and limits. That is what a budget does. It makes you conscious of the reality of how much you are spending or not saving.

Another important topic we will cover in this area of budgeting is debt. Debt can be one of the main reasons people can't save and invest. We're going to hit this head on and talk about the dangers of debt and how to get control.

In the third step, we will expand on the idea of creating a system to save and not just a goal and a number. As we will discuss, a goal takes discipline and discipline is in short supply for most of us. A system is something you do every day. You don't have to think about it, you do it habitually. A system can be a set it and forget it kind of thing. With a system, we use the power of habits and routine to give us momentum to the direction we desire.

Many times we know what is the right thing to do, it's just hard to maintain every day. That's why we want to harness the power of habit to drive us in the direction of financial success.

Step 1: Find an Income

Without an income, you will have nothing to save and invest. Pretty clear, pretty straight forward. For many people, an income comes from a job. This is true! But there are other methods to generate an income as well. An income can come from selling your time for money or it comes from creating something of value and selling the service or product you have created. This can give you leverage. This can give you the ability to hire others to help you. The product or service can also be created by someone else and you can leverage their experience.

We encourage entrepreneurship and business ownership. It can also help you develop skills you can use when you earn your financial freedom. It is kind of sad when people get to the point where they have financial freedom but don't know how to use their freedom.

This is more common than you think and we will discuss it more in the section on what to do after you have earned your freedom.

"My rich dad used to say, "you can never have true freedom without financial freedom". He would go on to say , "Freedom may be free, but it has a price."
– Robert Kiyosaki

Most of us have spent, or will spend, most of our lives working to improve our income. This can take many forms. The purpose of this book is not to talk about "how to" improve and grow your income.

It is our intent to encourage you to improve your income. Think about alternate sources of income. Build your skills. Begin to think about life when you don't "have to" work. Think about life when you are free to choose how to spend your time.

Start building those skills now. Start dreaming now.

There are a couple books that have been helpful to me. One is about knowing your strengths. This will help now and when you have more freedom.

The book is entitled *StrengthsFinder* (or *Now, Discover Your Strengths*). It was written by Marcus Buckingham and Donald O. Clifton and was first published in 2001. At the heart of the book is an online personal assessment test that will help you discover your strengths. The book talks about focusing on building strengths rather than focusing on weaknesses.

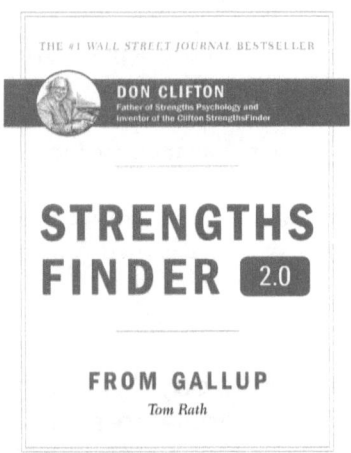

The theory behind the book is that each individual possesses a certain number of fixed universal personal-character attributes. These are "talent themes" which work together and result in an individual's tendency to develop certain skills more easily.

They have developed an online test that will reveal your top five talent themes. You can find it at www.strengthsfinder.com. This is a web based questionnaire will help you define your individual "Strengths".

Another book that was helpful to me was *What Color is Your Parachute?* by Richard Nelson Bolles. It is a book for job-seekers that has been in print since 1970 and has been revised every year since 1975. It is one of the most highly regarded career advice books in print.

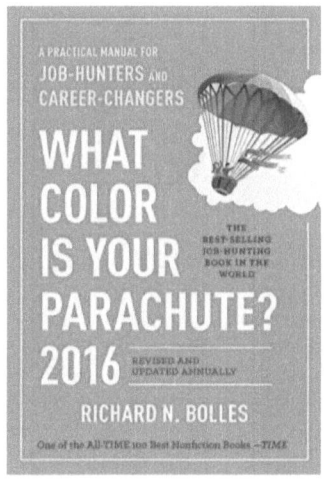

There are many interesting aspects to this book that will help you get a perspective on what you are good at and how you might enjoy spending your time. The exercises are great and I would encourage you to read it even if you are not looking for a job.

It is my hope that these recommendations will be helpful to you. Our next step will be to understand how this income is being spent in the form of expenses. Getting a handle on income and expenses in the form of a monthly budget is our next big step.

Step 2: Back to Basics: the monthly cash flow plan

Now that you have income, it's time to get an understanding of where all the money is going. You would think that financial budgets and keeping track of expenses would be a common skill among adult Americans. But, sadly, it is not. A key element to putting money in its proper place, in our hearts and minds, is understanding exactly what is happening with our money.

We have purposely avoided the word "budget". As with many things in the book, getting our minds to cooperate so we can behave in a way that helps us achieve our goals is a big part of the process. The word budget gets many people nervous. It is a word used in business environments or in situations where you are forced to stay on budget. We have used the term "cash flow plan" to better explain this step of the process.

Our purpose is to understand the flow of the cash in and out of your life. If we can get you to have a very clear understanding of where the money goes each month, you will have a better chance to make conscious decisions to alter your course of action.

Building a wealth is not a mystery, especially when understanding how your cash flow, flows every month.

The steps to doing this are pretty easy. The hard part is not the head knowledge, the hard part is putting your heart and mind into it. The issue with the mind is that it comes up with all the excuses for why this won't work for you.

It's real important to get past that and get your cash flow plan in writing. Things look different when you get it out of your head and onto paper. It also helps with our memories. We all have selective memory and unless we write it down, we will forget our plans and commitments.

In the area of cash flow planning and budgeting I recommend the program Dave Ramsey has put together. They have created an important process in this area. The forms and ideas are available for free online. He has also created a program called, "Financial Peace University". This is a 9-week program that you attend and work through all the planning issues. The cost of the program materials is currently $100.

Some people love this program, and some people hate it. Dave Ramsey has a very strong perspective on many things and it can get on some people's nerves. I understand this and I understand for some people this is an excuse to not take action. It is important for you to understand what is stopping you from making progress in this area. Don't be distracted from your goal of financial success. We highly recommend the process that Dave Ramsey offers.

If you are turned off by his perspective and antics, get the value from his teaching and move on. If attending a class is too intense, you can start by reading one of his books. After you get familiar with the topics, I highly recommend the class.

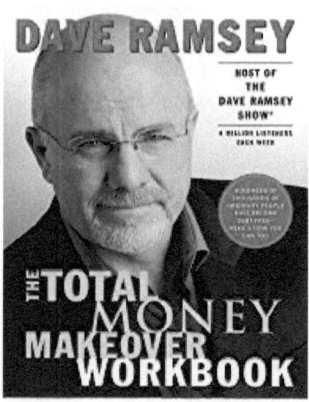

The place to start is the cash flow planning sheet. Here is a summary.

Budget Item	Planned to Spend	Actually Spent
CHARITABLE GIFTS		
SAVING		
Emergency Fund		
Retirement Fund		
College Fund		
HOUSING		
Mortgage		
Property Taxes		
Property Insurance		
Repairs		
Replace Furniture		
UTILITIES		
Electricity		
Water		
Gas		
Phone		
Garbage		
Cable		
Internet		
FOOD		
Groceries		
Restaurants		
TRANSPORTATION		
Car Payment		
Fuel		
Repairs / Tires		
Auto Insurance		
CLOTHING		
Children		
Adults		
MEDICAL / HEALTH		
Disability Insurance		
Health Insurance		
Doctor Bills		
Dentist		
Vitamins		
Medications		
PERSONAL		

Life Insurance	_____
Pocket Money	_____
Cosmetics / Hair	_____
Entertainment	_____
Vacation	_____
DEBTS	_____
Credit Cards	_____
Student Loans	_____
Other	_____
TOTAL	_____

Find this worksheet online by searching for "dave ramsey cash flow planning". You can also use the online tool they have created at https://www.everydollar.com/

One of the obstacles that will get in your way is how to handle weekly or bi-monthly income. When you get into this you will realize that as your income arrives each week, or so, you pay certain bills at different times of the month.

The "allocated spending plan" will help with this issue. Search for "dave ramey allocated spending plan" to find the detail. There are videos also that will help you understand how to use the allocated spending worksheet.

Another excuse many people come up with is that monthly cash flowing planning does not work for them because their income is too erratic. It comes in large sums at irregular intervals.

This is yet another excuse for not creating a cash flow plan. There are ways to address this that will help you relax and reduce stress and enjoy life. Open your mind. Think about it. Accountants and financial people have devised methods to address this issue.

Irregular income is very common for self-employed or commission-based salespeople. The first step is to create a budget. Search for "dave ramsey irregular income planning". Use the worksheet to list your expenses. Use the lowest-paid month from the previous year for the expected income. Set priorities for what will be paid in a low-income month.

There are many possible scenarios on how to deal with irregular income. The only unacceptable solution is to do nothing.

The emergency fund of 3 to 6 months of your gross income is critical in this situation. A cash buffer like this will help you smooth your income.

When you have this cash reserve you can pay yourself the minimum required to pay the bills.

If you are still confused and not able to make progress in this area, call me. I will help you.

Debt Elimination

The last topic to address is debt elimination. Debt is a constant issue for most people. There is a constant drumbeat in our society encouraging us to use debt. This is dangerous and out of control for many Americans.

If you want to have financial freedom, you cannot have debt. The idea of debt is known as bondage. You are bound until your debt is paid. That is the opposite of freedom. If you have ever had large debts handing over your head, you know what that feels like. As you near retirement or being financially free, this becomes an even more critical area to get under control.

A common tool used to eliminate debt is called the debt snowball. The idea is to list all your debts, smallest to largest. Payoff the small debts first, and do this regardless of interest rate. Work your way up the list until all the debts are paid. Start with the smaller debts first to get momentum and see progress.

This process is also useful because, many times, a list of all debts on a single page surprises people. This simple process is something they have never done. They did not realize how much debt they had. The first step in solving a problem is to gain understanding.

If you have followed Dave Ramsey at all, you will hear him refer people to Retirement Planning professionals. That is where I come in. This chapter has highlighted the strengths of the Financial Peace University program.

The weakness of this program is financial planning. Dave Ramsey understands this and works actively to connect people with financial planners.

What Dave Ramsey does is NOT financial planning. He is an expert in helping people setup a monthly cash flow plan and eliminate debt. He is exceptional at what he does. This is an important element to achieving your financial plans.

Next stop is, creating a savings system.

Step 3: Setup a System to Save

To achieve your goal to save money, the best way to do that is to setup a system. Why a system? A system is defined as a set of principles or procedures to which something is done, an organized scheme or method. Saving money is a big deal, and if you can't save money, there will be no reason to setup a financial plan. A system utilizes the best ideas to solve one of the biggest problems in saving money, HUMAN NATURE.

If you rely on your memory or your self-discipline, for most of us, we will fail. A goal takes discipline and discipline is in short supply. A system is something you do every day. You don't have to think about it, you do it habitually. A system can be a set it and forget it can of thing. With a system, we use the power of habits and routine to give us momentum to the direction we desire.

Create a system to ensure your savings will happen. If you don't it will be like the goal to lose 10 pounds. That is a great goal but unless you follow up with daily habits and routines, you will most likely not lose 10 pounds.

There are three reasons to save money. The first is to build cash reserves for emergencies. The second is to save for purchases, vacations, and cars. The third reason to save money is for wealth building. Cash reserves are setup for protection and defense against life's unexpected events. Cash reserves should NOT be in the same account where you pay your normal bills for gas and food. You need a separate account to preserve this money.

Cash reserves are for emergencies. You must define what your family considers "an emergency". If buying food and clothing is considered an emergency, something is not right.

Do not invest this money. Keep this money in a money market account. You may realize that a money market account pays very little in interest and that with inflation you are losing purchasing power. You would be correct BUT this cash reserve is a hedge against unexpected events. It is like insurance. You have to pay for insurance, right. Well, we advise you pay the price for the cash reserves.

REASONS to SAVE MONEY
1. Build Wealth
2. Save for a Purchase
3. Build cash reserves

The second reason to save money is to prepare for purchases. We advise that you save and buy stuff and not use debts. For example, if you want to buy a new couch, save the money first. If you want to buy a car, save the money first. If you want to repair the roof, save the money first. If you want to paint the house, save the money first.

Avoid DEBT ... it drains your resources.

Avoid credit card debt ... it will get out of control.

The last reason to save money is to build wealth for the future. This will build your ability to have future freedom. When it comes to saving money, the first thing most mention is the D word. The D word is discipline. I'd like to avoid discipline because, frankly, mine is not the good. And for most people, discipline is a nasty word.

Let's pursue a new approach. Let's put a system in place and let's work the system. In the case of money, the system will be making a decision, setting up the system, staying with it, and not stopping.

When it comes to building wealth, nothing is more important than a system. Wealth building is a marathon, not a sprint. That is why you must have a system. Building wealth really is not a mystery. It requires a plan and a system. This book is going to challenge your thinking when it comes to money. Most people think of money in isolated incidents. We want to start thinking in terms of your system and your plan.

A system is something that you do that increases your olds of success. A system is something you do day by day, week by week and month by month. If you do something every day, it's a system. Goals are a reach it and be done situation. A system is a way of life. Saving money must become a way of life.

Here is the savings system:

Step 1: Pick a number that you can deduct from your income every
time you get paid. Make the number so small that you don't have to think about it. You know you can deduct this amount of money and it will not be an issue. It does not matter at this point what the number is … just pick a number. Maybe five dollars, or 10 dollars or 100 dollars. The point is to setup the system before the resistance, fear, doubt, etc, can stop you.

Step 2: Create an account where you will move the money you have
deducted from your income. You can do this online. It will be best if you can setup automatic transfer from your income account to your savings account. Make sure that you can send money to this account automatically every pay period (without fees and expenses)

Step 3: Setup the auto transfer from your income account to your
savings account.

Step 4: Turn on the system and deduct the money and move it to your savings account.

Congratulations! You now have a savings system. The point of this exercise is to setup the system before all the doubts and fears and unanswered questions can stop you. This system is simple and there is a reason for the simplicity. We all make up tons of excuses why it is NOT possible. I just gave you a simple system to get you started in the right direction.

Don't get distracted by the amount you are saving. We will increase the amount later once we determine your income, expenses, debts and other financial responsibilities. Don't get distracted about whether it will be enough to retire, we will work this out later. Just start the system. Don't be distracted by the question of if the account should be a tax deferred account. Just start the system with a basic savings account. If we need to later, we can move the saved money to a tax deferred account. Don't get distracted about where to start the account. Just create the account with an bank or credit union you are already working with.

Now that you have created a system, it's now time to think about some safeguards around the system. Over time the system will create a very nice savings account. For many people, that money is in grave danger of being raided by pirates and bandits. I know that the bank is doing all they can to protect your money but a real danger exists that someone will try to take your savings. That person, that pirate, that bandit is YOU. You have to setup a system with safeguards to keep the pirate named _____(insert your name) from raiding this account.

As we will discuss a lot in this book, one of the biggest obstacles to our success is our own nature. Depending on who you are, you may need to setup safe guards to keep this money safe. Some of you may need to give the keys to this account to someone else. Tell them, that only under these specific circumstances will I be allowed to raid this money. This is called accountability and most of us need it a one level or another.

Another way to safe guard the money will be to move the money to retirement accounts. Retirement accounts have lots of rules and penalties to keep pirates like yourself from raiding the account. This does not stop everyone but it will stop a majority of people. This may be a good option for you and we will discuss this later.

As you come to know yourself, you may want to put other safeguards in place to keep bandits from raiding this account, in a moment of weakness.

Discipline is a precious resource. Use some of it now to create this saving system. You will need all the discipline you can muster for other areas of your life. Good luck!

Questions to Ponder

1. What is stopping me from saving?
2. How can I remove that obstacle to my freedom?
3. What is my vision for saving money and building wealth?
4. Does this vision motivate me or discourage me?
5. Do I need to modify my vision?
6. If your vision is not motivating me, how can I change it?

"One painful duty fulfilled makes the next plainer and easier."
— **Helen Keller**

"Do not train a child to learn by force or harshness; but direct them to it by what amuses their minds, so that you may be better able to discover with accuracy the peculiar bent of the genius of each."
— **Plato**

"The really important kind of freedom involves attention, and awareness, and discipline, and effort, and being able truly to care about other people and to sacrifice for them, over and over, in myriad petty little unsexy ways, every day."
— **David Foster Wallace**

"True freedom is impossible without a mind made free by discipline."
— **Mortimer J. Adler**

"By failing to prepare, you are preparing to fail."
– Benjamin Franklin

PART 2:
The Plan

A financial plan begins with a comprehensive assessment of your current situation. From this baseline, projections can be made based on future income, asset growth and time. As we all know, the future is uncertain but a plan can be very helpful in understanding the elements you can control.

There are definitely more variables that you cannot control about your future financial condition but the variables you can control are powerful. Some things you can focus on and control are income, education, and who you work with.

As with anything, the people you associate with regarding your finances will have a significant impact on your future. More on this later!

Education is critical. As a future wealthy person, you must have the knowledge to make decisions about your money and who you work with. If you don't educate yourself, you will not be able to make "educated" decisions. If you are currently wealthy, education will take you to the next level.

Many professional finance people talk about the accumulation phase and the distribution phase of a financial plan. The accumulation phase is the time when you are adding to your assets. This addition comes from income and the money you can save. Your income and saving rate is a major factor that you can control and it will have a significant impact on your financial plan.

The distribution phase is when you begin withdrawing money from your assets in the form of "income" and living expenses. This is traditionally known as retirement. We call it freedom. You are financially free when you can live off the assets you have accumulated and not worry about the money running out for a very long time, if ever.

The list of things you can't control is pretty large, I'd say infinite. From an economic perspective, inflation and interest rates are two things that will have a significant impact on your future. From a life perspective, the list is so long we won't go into it. (life, death, accidents, health, etc. etc. etc.)

From an investment perspective, you don't have direct control over the returns you will get from your assets. Education and experience can help a lot to improve your probabilities of success. Education and experience can also help you do better in reducing your taxes. At one level, you can't control the tax rate but there are strategies that can help.

Studies show that having a financial plan improves results. Makes sense, yet many people don't have a plan. Consider taking a road trip in the car to a destination you've never been before. The prudent thing to do would be to study and plan for the trip. How far away, how long will it take to drive, which road to the destination. Pretty simple. Same idea for a financial plan. If you've never been to the destination called financial success, create a plan. It will help.

In this book we are going to review the five pillars of a financial plan. For most people, when they think of a financial plan, they think about investments. Investments are only the first pillar.

The five pillars of a financial plan are:

1. Investment plan

2. Income plan

3. Insurance

4. Tax savings plan

5. Estate plan

If you are missing any one of these pillars, your financial future is at risk.

An investment plan includes all the things you'd expect. Stocks, bonds, cash, mutual funds, index funds, real estate, commodities, precious metals, gold.

- **What is an asset?** Anything of value that can be converted into cash. Examples of assets are real estate, stocks, bonds, cash, mutual funds, pensions, retirement plans. Assets tend to increase in value over time. (assets put money in your pocket)

- **What is a liability?** A financial debt or obligation. Examples of liabilities are mortgages, loans, and other obligations to pay. Liabilities tend to decrease in value over time. (liabilities take money out of your pocket)

- **What are stocks?** A share in the ownership of a company. If you think of a company like a cake, your share is your slice of the cake. Big companies have lots of shares (slices). Holding a company's stock means that you are one of the many owners (shareholders) of a company.

- **What are bonds?** A **bond** is a debt, similar to an IOU. Borrowers issue **bonds** to raise money from investors willing to lend them money for a certain amount of time. When you buy a **bond**, you are lending to the issuer, which may be a government, municipality, or corporation.

An income plan is not as familiar for most people. An income plan includes Social Security. Any pensions you've accumulated. And most importantly, how and when to withdraw money from your tax deferred accounts like a 401k account or an Individual Retirement Account (IRA).

Insurance comes in many forms and is very important to a successful financial plan. The purpose of insurance is to protect you from certain risks. When we discuss insurance we consider all forms: health insurance, auto insurance, life insurance, disability insurance. And several other types of insurance depending on your personal circumstances.

Taxes are an inevitable aspect of life and it's important to have a plan. Many of the investment accounts in your portfolio will have tax related rules. Not knowing these rule can be expense and, in some cases, catastrophic to your financial future. Keep in mind that we are not tax professionals. We seek out the best experts we can find in this area.

An estate plan includes trusts and wills. Understanding the importance of beneficiaries on your accounts is also a vital aspect of achieving your goals.

When you are considering your financial life, having a gap in one of these areas can carry significant consequences. You might have a solid investment plan but without the proper insurance, a major event could wipe out your investment portfolio. Without an estate plan, all that you create and saved during your lifetime can quickly be squandered. Not exactly what you want after a lifetime of labor.

Financial planning is complex and every situation carries differences. My concern for you, and the reason for this book, is that many times people don't know what they don't know. Hopefully this book can open your eyes and help you avoid some of the common traps.

Let's get started!

Investments: The Basics.

Investing is the process of putting your money to work for you. All the work you have done to save the money can now payoff. You have worked so hard to earn the money and now your money can work for you. Pretty cool deal. And when you have enough of those little dollars working for you, you will be free. You will have achieved financial freedom so that you can work on the projects that really interest you.

Investing and your investment plan are an important step. When most people think about financial planning, their first thought is about investments. This is an important step but the other pillars are vitally important as well. If you are missing any of these pillars, you have a weakness in your financial plan. Pay attention to all elements of the plan.

As your investments grow, you will achieve a state known as wealth. Wealth is simply an abundance of possessions or money. This state is achieved by living within your means and saving money. This is the first step. The second step is investing the money so that it will grow. The third step is, once the pot of money has grown, to protect the money.

SAVE – INVEST – PROTECT

What is the most important question to achieve financial freedom? Where am I going to put my money? Overwhelmingly, the most important aspect of investing is asset allocation.

Many people don't believe this. They think financial success is a luck thing only. Put all your money on red 8. Spin the wheel, just like at the casino. If you win, you win. If not, back to the salt mine. Not a wise strategy.

Asset Allocation is the most important investment decision of your lifetime. It is more important than any single investment you're going to make in stocks, bonds, real estate, or anything else. Just think about it in simple terms. Your wealth is determined by where you put your money and in what proportion.

Asset Allocation is a big fancy term, but what does it mean? Asset allocation is the process of spreading your money into different buckets. You've heard the term "don't put all your eggs in one basket", that is asset allocation. Or egg allocation.

The buckets/baskets are stocks, bonds, cash, real estate, commodities, and precious metals. Your success as an investor depends on the allocation of your money into these buckets.

The very next question is, how much money should I put into each basket? We are getting ahead of ourselves, but the proportion into each basket depends on what is happening in the economy, inflation, interest rates, and markets around the world.

Portfolio Allocation

The buckets / baskets include:

- **Stocks**
- **Bonds**
- **Cash**
- **Commodities**
- **Gold**

There are other buckets you could add but this is a starting point. Within each bucket there are other buckets (like Russian nesting dolls)

- Stocks might include …
    - US Domestic stocks
    - International stocks
    - Emerging market stocks
    - Large cap stocks
    - Mid cap stocks
    - Small cap stocks
    - Value stocks
    - Growth stocks

Each of the big buckets listed above have many investment options within them. The way you allocate to these is crucial to your success. Asset allocation can get complicated when you get into the details. At the top level, it is very simple to explain (eggs in a basket), but implementation can be very hard. There is a lot of detail and information to process before you become proficient at the process.

As you know, I work with lots of people in various stages of life. Some are retired, some are employees of large companies. For the majority, most people are not that interested in the details of investing. Most don't know the difference between the S&P 500 and the Russell 2000. This is not necessarily bad, but if you are investing by yourself you would need to know this.

I recommend getting professional help when it comes to managing your money. There are many reasons for this, as we will discuss later. But I hope you are starting to see how important knowledge is to the process of investing.

Before we get into more detail on asset allocation, let's return to some basic ideas that inform our investing ideas.

Individual Stocks and Bonds, Markets and Indexes

Now that you have some understanding of the buckets involved in asset allocation, we can discuss what goes into each of these buckets.

You can buy individual securities like stocks or bonds. (see definition of each in prior section) Or you can buy individual assets like real estate or gold. But before you make that leap, consider a safer way.

In the investment world, they are constantly doing research on the best way to invest and make money. In 1973 a book was written by Burton Malkiel called "A Random Walk Down Wall Street". In that book, the author, a Princeton economist, makes the argument that asset prices appear to exhibit signs of a "random walk" and that one cannot consistently beat market averages.

This book set off a raging argument that has lasted for the last thirty years. The argument has been over which management strategy is the best, active management or index management. (Index management is sometimes called passive management.) Active management is when a highly paid investment professional studies the stocks and bonds they think are the best. They put money into the investments based on their judgment and selection.

Index management is the process of just buying the stocks or bonds in an index. An index could be the 500 largest publically traded stocks. Or it could be the 2000 small publically traded stocks. Or it could be U.S. Treasury bonds with a duration over 20 years. There are lots of index to choose from.

This is a mechanical process and can be performed by a computer. This management style eliminates the need for the highly paid professional. This management style has lower expenses and lower expenses means more money for the investor.

Now you may be asking, what is an index? The most famous index is the Standard & Poor's 500. The S&P 500 is a list of the 500 largest publically traded companies in the US. Another famous index is the Dow Jones Industrial Average. This is a handpicked list of 30 large US companies.

(Technically the Dow Jones Industrial Average is not an index but is used like one)

As this debate has raged, more and more indexes have been created. There are indexes of small company stocks. Indexes of US Treasury Bonds. Indexes of tech companies, or energy companies, or … you name it.

What the research has confirmed over the last 30 years is that active managers do not beat the indexes, they are measured against, on a long-term basis. This is very significant. Investors have noticed and have moved their money to passive index funds.

Today the largest fund in the world is the Vanguard Total Stock Market Index. It is four times larger than the next largest actively managed fund. Needless to say, I do not recommend individual stocks or bonds. I primarily recommend index funds. Although, there are some limited circumstances where I do use actively managed funds.

Our asset allocation process and the creation of our portfolios use indexes of market segments to achieve our results. These decisions allow us to do three really important things …

1. Produce investment results
2. Control risks
3. Control costs

We have talked about how active managers struggle to beat their index. We have decided to invest in the index and achieve performance that matches the index. A good solid decision.

What we have not talked about is how asset allocation helps us reduce risk. In life, risk can come in many forms. In the section on insurance, we will talk about how we use insurance to manage this risk.

RISK

Here in the section on investments, we define risk as the chance an investment's actual return will differ from the expected return. In simple terms, what is the chance I will lose money? No investment is without risk but we want to reduce the chances of losing money.

In math terms, we measure risk by looking at the standard deviation. The standard deviation is what I call "the wiggle". When you look at a chart of a stock or an index, you will see the jagged line that shows the historical price movement of the security. This line "wiggles" up and down, day by day.

Some stocks and some markets wiggle, or move up and down more than others. We use various types of assets to counter balance each other. This allocation reduces the risk of losing. This has been mathematically and scientifically proven and I will not go into it here. But keep in mind, our decision to use indexes versus individual securities reduced our risk of losing in a single stock. And now, we are risking our risk further by counter-balancing the risks of various types of investments.

All of this is well and good but the most important aspect of risk control is the mindset of the investor. The reason we want to reduce the wild swings of an investment is because most people can't take the gut wrenching feeling of losing money. We will cover this in more detail in the section on mindset, but risk control is an important element in keeping your mind and head in the game. Keeping your head in the game is the only way to achieve long-term results.

Before we leave this topic, many people believe that risk control reduces your ability to perform well (i.e. make money). They believe you have to buy the riskiest investment possible and close your eyes. This is back to the idea of getting lucky and placing all your money on red 8 at the roulette table.

Reducing risk can allow you to win over the long term. We can show the benefits of not going into a big hole (losing a lot of money) and taking the big market swings. This is counter-intuitive, but can be shown to be the best way to grow your money and keep your money. Asset allocation is the way.

The third important thing we are able to do is control costs. As we talked about in the section on active investing, our method allows us the keep costs low. We do this by using index funds. The pressure to reduce fees has been one of the side benefits of the move to index investing. This is a good thing for you, the investor.

Let's return now to more detail on asset allocation.

More Ways to Allocation Your Money

Now that we have talked about some of the basics of what goes into a portfolio, let's talk now about some of the ways to allocate your money. Keep in mind that the ideas in this book are not new or unique to me. The ideas in the book are things I have found and learned in my search for investing success.

Ray Dalio is one of those people I have found and that I listen to for his wisdom in the world of investing. He is a giant in the investment world. He is the founder of one of the largest investment funds in the world.

Asset allocation is his expertise and he is a teacher at heart. He is recognized around the world for his investment process and ability to build portfolios that perform well in all economic seasons.

The ideas in this book, relating to asset allocation, come from Ray and his experiences at Bridgewater Associates. They manage risk better than most. The success of his company makes it very difficult for "normal" people to gain access to his expertise. In recent years, if you have been paying attention, his knowledge has begun to be published in a number of ways. We can be the beneficiary of this access.

My hope is that we can take what we have learned about a complex subject, like asset allocation, and make it simple enough to act on. It doesn't matter if you have $1,000 to invest or $1 million. The principles are critical to getting you to the next level.

Asset allocation is the one key skill that can set you apart from 99% of all investors. Asset allocation is known as "the only free lunch" in investing. Why is this? Because spreading your money around decreases your risk, increases our upside returns, and doesn't cost you anything.

We all know of the horror stories of putting all your money in one company. For a while, you might be flying high. But what happens when the stock drops 40%. Ouch.

Asset allocation offers you a set of guiding principles and a philosophy of investing. Each asset bucket will have different characteristics of risk and reward.

We have discussed the starting point of asset allocation. Let's go deeper.

Here are some sample portfolios

A traditional portfolio might have a stock and bond split like this: 80% stocks and 20% bonds. The split could be 60% stock and 40% bonds. Or 20% stocks and 80% bonds. The percentage split could be modified based on age or tolerance for risk. This is the traditional approach.

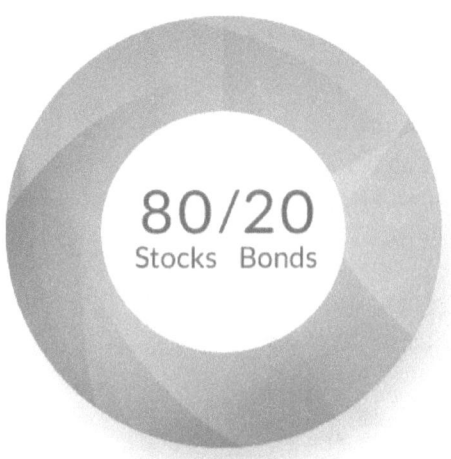

80/20
Stocks Bonds

As you will see, most of the risk lies with the stocks. The thinking goes, if you want less risk, lower the stock allocation. There are a few other asset classes missing from this allocation. Even our simple allocation is missing cash, commodities and precious metals.

As you will recall, we strive to manage risk as well. An allocation like this puts a high level of risk in the portfolio. In a 50/50 split of stocks and bonds, 95% of the risk lies with the stocks.

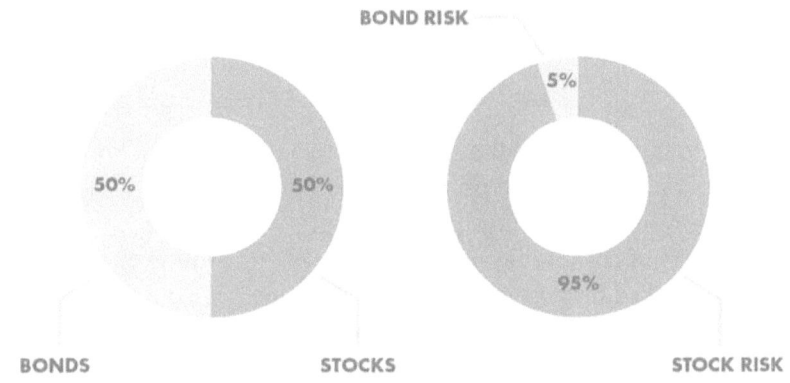

BOND RISK

5%

50%   50%

95%

BONDS   STOCKS   STOCK RISK

This means a portfolio like this will follow the swings of the stock market very closely. Remember standard deviation and "the wiggle". If you compare of chart of the S&P 500 and a 50/50 stock/bond portfolio, it will follow all-stock index very closely.

Here's another sample portfolio recommended by the David Swenson, the manager for the Yale University endowment. David is the manager of a $25 billion dollar fund. Here is the portfolio he recommends.

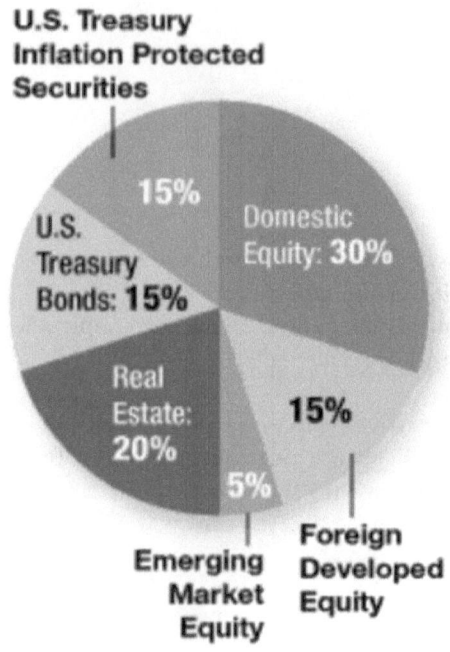

- **Domestic Equity (30 percent)**
  Stocks of U.S. based publically traded companies.
- **Emerging Market Equity (5 percent)**
  Stocks of companies in emerging markets around the world. Places like Brazil, Russia, India and China.
- **Foreign Developed Equity (15 percent)**
  Stocks of companies in foreign developed countries like the United Kingdom, Germany, France and Japan.
- **Real Estate Investment Trusts (20 percent)**
  Stocks of companies that invest directly in real estate properties.

- **U.S. Notes and Bonds (15 percent)**
  These are fixed-interest U.S. government debt securities.
- **U.S. Treasury Inflation-Protection Securites, or TIPS (15 percent)**
  These are special types of Treasury notes that offer protection from inflation.

A portfolio like this performs much differently than the simple 50/50 stock bond split we discussed above. Some of the things that really change the result is the allocation to real estate, TIPS, foreign and emerging market equities.

Here is a portfolio recommended by Ray Dalio. It is the called the All Seasons portfolio.

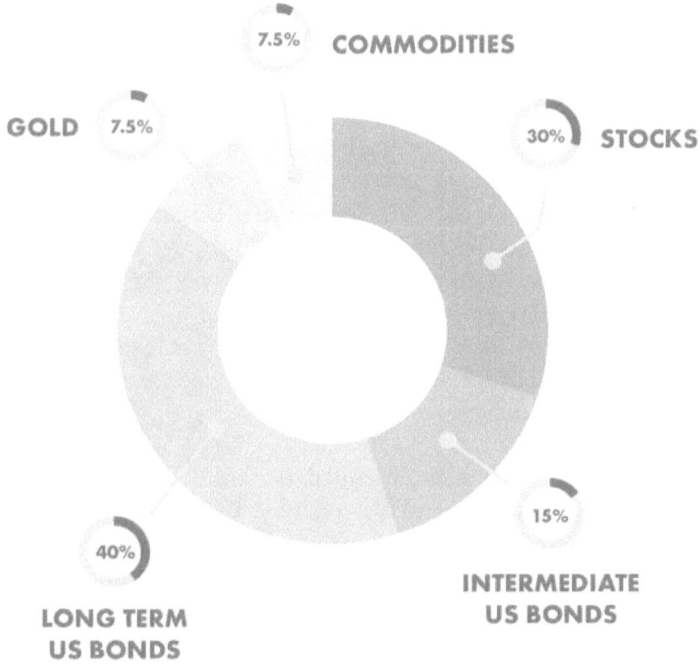

As you can see, the allocation to stocks is very small, only 30 percent. It has an allocation to a basket of commodities like corn, sugar, cattle, etc. It includes gold but not other precious metals. And a large allocation to U.S. bonds.

Now, why do they call it "All Seasons"? Just as there are seasons each calendar year, there are seasons and cycles to investments. According to Dalio, there are only **four things that move the price of assets**:
1. **Inflation**
2. **Deflation**
3. **Rising economic growth**
4. **Declining economic growth**

And, there are only four different possible environments, or economic seasons, that will ultimately affect whether investments (asset prices) go up or down. (Unlike nature, however, there is not a predetermined order in which the seasons will arrive.)

These **seasons** are:

1. Higher than expected inflation (rising prices)
2. Lower than expected inflation (or deflation)
3. Higher than expected economic growth
4. Lower than expected economic growth

Because there are only four potential economic environments or seasons, Dalio says you should have 25% of your *risk* in each of these four categories. That's why he calls this approach All Seasons. There are four possible seasons in the financial world, and nobody really knows which season will come next. With this approach, each season, each quadrant, is covered all the time, so you're always protected.

As we have discussed, the application of these principles are harder to implement than to understand. Within each bucket there are questions to be answered about specifics.

For example, when each recommended portfolio talks about stocks, or domestic equities, which stocks do you buy. We have talked in the past about not buying individual stocks but using indexes. There are many indexes to choose.

For example, the S&P 500 is divided into 11 sectors. You can buy the stocks within each sector. How do you decide which sector to favor?

11 S&P 500 Sectors

1. Technology
2. Energy
3. Financials
4. Industrial
5. Consumer Non-Cyclical
6. Telecom
7. Basic Materials
8. Consumer Cyclical
9. Utilities
10. Healthcare
11. Real Estate

Here is a list of some of the most popular stock indexes.

Stock Indexes

- **Global**
    - MSCI World
    - S&P Global 100
    - S&P Global 1200
    - Russell Global
    - The Global Dow - Global version of the Dow Jones Industrial Average
    - Dow Jones Global Titans 50
    - Dow Jones Global Total Stock Market Index
    - FTSE All-World index series
- **Regional indices**
    - MSCI EAFE (Europe, Australasia, and Far East)
    - Asia
    - S&P Asia 50
    - Dow Jones Asian Titans 50 Index

- o Dow Jones Asia/Pacific Small-Cap Total Stock Market Index (DWAPS)
- o Europe
- o EURO STOXX 50 - 50 large blue chip companies in the Eurozone
- o FTSE Eurotop 100 - 100 most highly capitalised blue chip companies in Europe
- o Latin America
- o S&P Latin America 40
- o Southeast Asia
- o FTSE/ASEAN 40
- o FTSE/ASEAN

- **National indices**
  We are not going to list all the National indices here. Just keep in mind that every country in the world has an index to represent the stocks within the country.

- **United States**
  - Amex indices
  - NYSE Arca Major Market Index
  - Amex Volatility Index
  - Amex Composite Index
  - Amex Gold Miners Index
  - CBOE indices
  - CBOE DJIA BuyWrite Index (BXD)
  - CBOE NASDAQ-100 BuyWrite Index (BXN)
  - CBOE NASDAQ-100 Volatility Index (VXN)
  - CBOE S&P 500 BuyWrite Index (BXM)
  - CBOE Volatility Index (VIX)
  - Dow Jones & Company indices

- Dow Jones Industrial Average

- Dow Jones Transportation Average

- Dow Jones Utility Average

- Dow Jones U.S. Large Cap Growth Index

- Dow Jones U.S. Large Cap Value Index

- Dow Jones U.S. Small Cap Growth Index

- Dow Jones U.S. Small Cap Value Index

- Dow Jones U.S. Total Market Index

- Dow Jones U.S. Select Dividend Index

- Dow Jones U.S. Sector Indexes

- Dow Jones U.S. Target Date Indexes

- Goldman Sachs indices

- GSTI Semiconductor Index

- GSTI Software Index

- MSCI indices

- US LARGE CAP 300 INDEX

- US LARGE CAP VALUE

- US LARGE CAP GROWTH

- US MID CAP 450 INDEX

- US MID CAP VALUE

- US MID CAP GROWTH

- US SMALL CAP 1750 INDEX

- US SMALL CAP VALUE

- US SMALL CAP GROWTH

- Nasdaq indices

- NASDAQ Composite

- NASDAQ-100
- NASDAQ Volatility Index
- Russell Indexes (published by Russell Investment Group)
- Russell 3000
- Russell 3000 Growth
- Russell 3000 Value
- Russell 1000
- Russell 1000 Growth
- Russell 1000 Value
- Russell 2000
- Russell 2000 Growth
- Russell 2000 Value
- Russell Top 200
- Russell Top 200 Growth
- Russell Top 200 Value
- Russell MidCap
- Russell MidCap Growth
- Russell MidCap Value
- Russell 2500
- Russell 2500 Growth
- Russell 2500 Value
- Russell Small Cap Completeness
- Russell Small Cap Completeness Growth
- Russell Small Cap Completeness Value
- Standard & Poor's indices

- S&P 500 (GSPC,INX,SPX)

- S&P Midcap 400

- S&P SmallCap 600

- Value Line Composite Index

- Wilshire Associates indices

- Wilshire 5000

- Wilshire 4500

- Wilshire US REIT

- Wilshire US RESI

- Wilshire US Large Cap

- Wilshire US Large Cap Growth

- Wilshire US Large Cap Value

- Wilshire US Mid Cap

- Wilshire US Mid Cap Growth

- Wilshire US Mid Cap Value

- Wilshire US Small Cap

- Wilshire US Small Cap Growth

- Wilshire US Small Cap Value

- Wilshire US Micro Cap

- Wilshire Global REIT

- Wilshire Global RESI

- Wilshire Global REIT ex US

- Wilshire Global RESI ex US

This is an amazing list. It shows the growth of the index idea. Thirty years ago, who could have imagined the explosion of indices. And this is just for stocks. It does not include bonds or commodities.

In the bond world, there are lots of indexes to choose from. You can buy bonds with each of these areas. How do you decide which bonds to favor?

Bond Indexes

- **Global**
    - o (Bank of America) Merrill Lynch Global Bond Index
    - o Barclays Capital Aggregate Bond Index
    - o Citi World Broad Investment-Grade Bond Index (WorldBIG)
- **U.S. Bonds**
    - o (Bank of America) Merrill Lynch Domestic Master
    - o (Barclays) Lehman Brothers US Treasury Index
    - o the Capital Markets Bond Index
    - o Citi US Broad Investment-Grade Bond Index (USBIG)
- **Government Bonds**
    - o Barclays Inflation-Linked Euro Government Bond Index
    - o Citi World Government Bond Index (WGBI)
    - o FTSE UK Gilts Index Series
    - o J.P. Morgan Government Bond Index
- **Emerging Market Bonds**
    - o J.P. Morgan Emerging Markets Bond Index
    - o Citi Emerging Markets Broad Bond Index (EMUSDBBI)
- **High-Yield Bonds**
    - o (Bank of America) Merrill Lynch High-Yield Master II

- o   Barclays High-Yield Index
- o   Bear Stearns High-Yield Index
- o   Citi US High-Yield Market Index
- o   (Credit Suisse) First Boston High-Yield II Index
- o   S&P US Issued High-Yield Corporate Bond Index

- **Leveraged Loans**
    - o   S&P Leveraged Loan Index

Are you overwhelmed yet? There are many important decisions to make in the area of asset allocation.

Let's return to our fundamentals. We want to build a portfolio with baskets of stock, bonds, cash, and commodities. If we choose one of the sample portfolios above, like the All Seasons, we can populate the baskets with the indices for each.

Here is how you could build an All-Seasons portfolio using Exchange Traded Funds (ETFs).

Symbol	Name	Price	Weight
$DJUBS	Bloomberg Commodity Index	86.29	7.5%
$CASH	CASH	1.00	1%
TLH	iShares 10-20 Year Treasury Bond	131.87	10%
SHY	iShares 1-3 Year Treasury Bond	84.34	5%
TLT	iShares 20+ Year Treasury Bond	118.05	15%
IEI	iShares 3-7 Year Treasury Bond	121.94	7%
IEF	iShares 7-10 Year Treasury Bond	103.96	7%
AGG	iShares Core US Aggregate Bond	107.42	5%
IWM	iShares Russell 2000	136.04	10%
TLO	SPDR® Blmbg Barclays Long Term Trs ETF	68.43	5%
GLD	SPDR® Gold Shares	107.93	7.5%
SPY	SPDR® S&P 500 ETF	225.71	20%

We are not going to discuss the performance of this portfolio over the last 80 years but it is very acceptable indeed. If you are interested in the performance, contact me directly at marshall@clarionadvisors.com.

We've covered lots of details in this section on the basics of investing. As you can see, it is simple in concept but can get complicated in the implementation.

There are a couple other ideas I want to address before we close this section on investing.

Real Estate

We have broken real estate out into a separate bucket because real estate is unique for many reasons. For the individual investor, their home is a large asset relative to the other assets they own. It is also a shelter for themselves and their families.

A home is both an asset and a liability. It is an asset because it has value and can be converted into cash. (although it can take a while). A home is also a liability. If you have a mortgage, it is counted against the value of the property. And real estate will always have maintenance counts.

The most important thing about your home is that it is important to reduce the liabilities as much as you can as you get close to financial freedom (known by some as retirement). The best way to do this is to pay off your mortgage. Then the only liability will be the maintenance costs. This will allow you financial freedom and power.

Some of your may own second homes or rental properties. We are not going to get into a lot of detail on this other than to say, reduce debts and keep them low. And zero debt is the best debt number of them all.

Annuities

Annuities are a part of your investments but their characteristics are very different. We consider annuities an alternative to cash. They are the safe money bucket. They are guaranteed by an insurance company.

An annuity is a contract between you and an insurance company. You enter this contract for the benefits it provides to your financial plan. Before we get into the benefits, it's important to understand the types of annuities available.

Types of annuities
- Fixed
- Indexed
- Variable

A fixed annuity is much like a certificate of deposit (CD). The contract you sign with the insurance company "guarantees" you a fixed rate of return for a specific period of time. Keep in mind that insurance companies are competing for the money with banks. Many times the rates are higher for fixed annuities than for CDs.

An important distinction regarding annuities is whether they are immediate or deferred. An immediate annuity starts paying an income right now (immediately). A deferred annuity grows in value over time and income is started at some future date.

An index annuity generates returns based on a specific equity-based index. That's right, annuity returns guaranteed by an insurance company but based on the performance of a stock index. Pretty cool.

These annuities usually are guaranteed to never go below zero even if the stock market returns are negative. This is called the floor. Sometimes the floor can be one percent or higher. It depends on market conditions.

On the top side, an index-annuity has a cap. This means that if the stock market returns 12% in one year, the cap may be 6%. You would get 6% and the insurance company would get the difference. This is one way insurance company makes money. They guarantee you from loses but take the upside. This can be a very good deal for some portion of your portfolio. In 2008 and 2009, many clients had index annuity and they were very glad they did.

A variable annuity offer investors the opportunity to get an insurance company guarantee and invest in stocks and bonds through subaccounts. I consider a variable annuity a chance to invest in a mutual fund with a annuity wrapper. There are various guarantees with these products have related to income you can't outlive, death benefits, and guarantees against loss of principle.

Variable annuities are very popular and many people buy them every year. We do not recommend these because of the complexity and cost. Many other smart people, and experts, in the field do not recommend variable annuities.

My best advice on variable annuities is to seek good advice and make sure the advisor is not biased by the large commission that is available on these products. There are some circumstances where this might make sense but you must keep a close eye on expenses and the quality of the insurance company.

KEY QUESTION: How Much Do I Need To Save and Invest to Be Financially Free?

The simple answer is that it depends on your lifestyle and expenses. A good rule is thumb is to save and invest 10% of your income. If you reach 15% of income, everything starts looking fantastic.

This may not seem realistic for you now but it can become realistic if you are willing to work at it. The combination of saving and investing will make you financially free. It is possible and it starts by believing it is possible.

We see many people living free. They way they did it was by saving and investing.

Here is another, more detailed, way to answer this question. If you start with your current income and work backward it might look something like this.

- Your current income is $60,000 a year before taxes.

- Your take home after taxes is $48,000. (these are really rough numbers).
- Your income in retirement (or financial freedom) is 80% of 48,000
- Your monthly income needs are $3200 (80% of 48,000, and then divided by 12)
- Your monthly Social Security payment for you and your spouse are $2000
- Your monthly income need after Social Security is $1200 a month
- If your investments generate 5% a year, you will need $300,000 to generate $1250 a month
- If your investments generate 10% a year, you will need $150,000 to generate $1250 a month
- If your investments generate 12% a year, you will need $120,000 to generate $1200 a month.

The answer to this question is complicated. This is a simple way to determine how much you need to save and investment to achieve financial freedom.

If you are not close, let's get started today.

KEY QUESTION: When Do I Shift Assets Among the Buckets?

This is a great question. And a very important question. As you have seen, there are seasons and times to change your investment balances within the buckets. Sometimes this is called "your tilt". Based on market and economic conditions, you may tilt your percentages up or down within each bucket.

We will talk about this more in the next section but the short answer is to base these shifts on rules, not emotions. One common rule based approach to shifting assets among buckets is called rebalancing.

Rebalancing is the process of automatically shifting assets of a portfolio. Rebalancing involves periodically buying or selling assets in a portfolio to maintain an original desired level of asset allocation.

For example, say an original target asset allocation was 50% stocks and 50% bonds. If the stocks performed well during the period, it could have increased the stock weighting of the portfolio to 70%. The investor may then decide to sell some stocks and buy bonds to get the portfolio back to the original target allocation of 50/50.

This type of rule-based approach is smart and support by tons of scientific research. It adds to your overall performance to do this rebalancing on a regular basis, regardless of how you "feel" about the markets.

The other part of this question is when do I change the allocation or percentage of assets dedicated to each bucket? That is a big big question. We refer back to the sample portfolios but there seasons and times when we expand or contract buckets.

MINDSET

The most important element to financial success is how you think about money. There, I said it. It all starts with how you think. You might not believe this but my statement is based in science and not just my opinion.

There is a field called behavioral economics. It is the study of psychology as it relates to the economic decision making processes of individuals and institutions. **Behavioral finance** is a relatively new field that seeks to combine **behavioral** and cognitive psychological theory with conventional economics and **finance.** The goal of this field is to provide explanations for why people make the decisions they make. Why are some financial decisions are irrational and some are not. What is driving these investment decisions? You'd think pure logic drives the world but it does NOT.

As you may realize, there is a lot of drama and emotion related to money. Think about your own personal life. The drama and emotion can escalate as the sums of money increase. This escalation goes from the individual investor to the global economic system (including all individuals and decision makers). Can you see how this field is important to understand? Can you see how a good understanding of our own investment process and decision-making can help us make better decisions? I hope you can.

As with most things, I like to return to fundamental, founding principles. In the 1960s cognitive psychology began to shed more light on the brain as an information processing device (in contrast to behaviorist models). Psychologists in this field, such as Amos Tversky, and Daniel Kahneman began to compare their cognitive models of decision-making under risk and uncertainty.

They came to realize the psychological biases inherit in humans. Biases are human tendencies that lead us to follow a particular quasi-logical path, or form a certain perspective based on predetermined mental notions and beliefs. When investors act on a bias, they do not explore the full issue and can be ignorant to evidence that contradicts their initial opinions. Avoiding cognitive biases allows investors to reach impartial decision based solely on available data.

There are several great books that explore this topic and make it accessible to non-academics. The first is "**Misbehaving: The Making of Behavior Economics**" written by Richard H. Thaler. He has been a contributor and observer of the field since its inception. The book is a history and summary of the topic.

The second new book on the topic is written by Michael Lewis and titled "**The Undoing Project: A Friendship that Changed Our Minds**". Michael Lewis is my favorite writer and the author of many bestsellers including "The Big Short", "The Blind Side", "Moneyball", and "Liar's Poker".

The book is the story of Amos Tversky and Daniel Kahneman who, in 1979, wrote the breakthrough paper in this field. Both had important careers in the Israeli military and became one of the great partnerships in the history of science

Their initial paper, "Prospect Theory: An Analysis of Decision under Risk," was about how people handle uncertain rewards and risks. In the ensuing decades, it became one of the most widely cited papers in economics. The authors argued that the ways in which alternatives are *framed* heavily influence the decisions people make. This was a seminal paper in behavioral economics.

Some common psychological biases plaguing investors include:

- Confirmation bias
  - Acknowledging confirmatory evidence while ignoring contradictory evidence
- Loss aversion bias
  - Disliking losses more than liking gains
- Representative bias
  - Stereotyping or "pigeonholing" someone or something and assuming that because someone or something shares one characteristic with a group of people/things, they share all of the characteristics of that group.
- Home bias
  - The tendency of investors to invest in domestic assets and avoid foreign assets, despite the benefits.
- Familiarity bias
  - A tendency to stay with what you know and avoid what you don't know.
- Mood and optimism bias
  - Mood is a big determinate in how we invest. And many times are moods lead us down the wrong path.
- Overconfidence bias
  - A well-established bias in which a person's subjective confidence in their judgments is greater than the objective accuracy of those judgments, especially when confidence is high.
- Endowment effects
  - People ascribe more value to things simply because the own them.
- Status Quo bias
  - A preference for doing nothing or maintaining the current state of affairs.
- Law of small numbers bias
  - The tendency for a initial segment of data to show some bias that drops out later.

- Mental accounting bias
  - When people put their money in two separate categories, or mental accounts. Also known as the "two-pocket" theory. This causes misrepresentation and not an actual accounting.
- Changing risk preference
  - As markets and moods change, the risk preference can change.
- Herd instinct
- Self-attribution bias
  - Tendency to attribute success to personal skills and failures to factors beyond their control.
- Availability bias
  - Judging outcomes by previous experiences of similar outcomes.
- Disposition effect
  - Selling investments after little gains but hanging on to them even after significant losses.

These biases, or mental shortcuts, lead to irrational investment decisions. They have their place and purpose in nature but can lead you astray. This understanding, at a collective level, gives a clearer explanation of why bubbles and panics occur. As investors and portfolio manager, we have a vested interest in understanding behavioral finance.

Making better investment decisions is what investment success is all about. It is my hope that this section has highlighted some of the important mental aspects of investing. Without this perspective, it is easy to get caught in emotional traps that make you do the wrong thing at the wrong time.

We use many tools to help us make better decisions. In this chapter we have highlighted a few. Asset allocation, market indexes, and mental preparation all play a part in getting us closer to that elusive goal.

Let's turn our attention now to Income Planning.

SECTION 2:

Income Planning

Income planning is the process of creating a detailed strategy for determining how much income you'll need to live the retirement lifestyle you want. From this you need to come up with a realistic way to generate that income. Income planning is really similar to the work we did for creating a cash flow plan (sometimes called a budget). This process is about looking at plans for the future and how you want to live in the future.

Some people consider moving to reduce expenses, some people want to travel. All of this is part of the income planning step. You have saved and have money in 401k accounts or IRA accounts or Roth IRA accounts or investment accounts. How do your turn your savings into income? And how much income will you need to live the lifestyle you want? These are the important questions of income planning.

As with anything related to the future, it is uncertain and planning is only our best guess at how things will be when you convert your savings into income.

It is never too early to consider income planning. Income can come from your assets you have created by your savings, or from a pension you received from a company, government or union. And then, income comes to every American from Social Security. Thinking about this income early in your career is a great idea. Not because you want to retire but because you want freedom. (the theme of this book ... Future Freedom)

We use a simple three-step plan. The good news is that coming up with a retirement income plan, whether on your own or with the help of an advisor, isn't impossible. It helps if you give yourself plenty of lead time. You can boil it down to the essentials by following these three key steps.

1. **Estimate how much income you will need.**
2. **Determine the sources of the income**
3. **Start with a reasonable withdrawal rate – and be prepared to change it.**

When you break things down to simple steps it will help you take the first step. The idea of planning your income for the next 25 years can be overwhelming. Taking one little baby step is easy.

Let's get stared.

STEP 1:
Estimate How Much Income You Will Need

One simple way to determine the income you need is to take a percentage of your current income as a starting point. For example, let's say you start with 80% of your current income as the income you will need in retirement. The expectation is that you will need less money in retirement because all you children are grown and out of the house (hopefully) and your debts are all paid (including your house, hopefully).

Let's say your current income is $5,000 a month, 80% of that is $4,000. This would mean that you need $4,000 in income.

You can adjust the percentage up or down based on your current situation. 70% of $5,000 is $3,500. 90% of $5,000 is $4,500. You get the idea.

There are much more complicated ways to determine your income needsbut this works for now. A survey recently found that fewer than four in ten Americans had tried to translate their assets into retirement income. If you do this, you will be in top of your class. (every little bit helps) When you get closer to retirement it might make sense to get a more detailed review of the income you will need to cover your expenses.

We are assuming your expenses will be lower when you start drawing income. There are some circumstances where this may not be the case. This is where the planning comes in. Better to know now than after you have started drawing income.

The best way to determine your needs for income and get a handle on what you spending will be is to use the cash flow plan we discussed earlier in this book.

STEP 2:
Determine The Sources Of Income

When it comes to income planning the word "guarantee" gets used a lot. The reason for this is the need to assure people they will have the income they need so they never run out of money. As you know from our discussions about the future, nothing is ever certain. Be careful about how much faith you put in the word "guarantee".

The first source people consider "guranteed" is Social Security. Social Security is a promise from the U.S. government that it will pay its citizens an income until the end of their lives. Some people question whether this is true given the level of debt the U.S. government has incurred.

In my prior book, I have covered this in detail. The short version is that when Social Security was created in 1935, the life expectancy for a man was 58 and 62 for a women. The full retirement age for Social Security was 65. That's right. To age to qualify for Social Security was above the expected life of most citizens. It was a program for those who attained "old age". The program was created with the expectation that a high percentage of the population would never need the money.

What has happened in the last 80 years is that life expectancy has soared. The retirement age for Social Security is 67. Life expectancy for the general population is 78. This means that a very high percentage of the population will need payments from the program. (*CYNICISM ALERT*) My cynical side says that someone in the government realized that if they did not change the Social Security retirement age, every American citizen would be a dependent of the state. Every American would expect the government to support them in old age. And that is exactly what has happened for a very high percentage of Americans. A pretty cool trick to make everyone dependent on the government. Very cool .

The solution, of course, is to raise the retirement age for young people who have 40 or 50 years to prepare for the changes in Social Security. Simple solution, a bunch of bad politicians.

So to answer the question, "will Social Security be around when I need it?" The answer is yes, in some form. Let's hope the politicians make a change before something catastrophic happens. (not hopeful of that)

A second source people consider "guaranteed" is a pension from a state or local government. This can include public employee unions. In California, this would be CalPERS, CalSTRS, etc.

A third source considered "guaranteed" is income from an insurance company. This can come in the form of annuities payments. We discussed annuities in the section on investments. The income you can generate from an annuity can be very helpful in retirement.

We recommend that you work with a professional who knows annuities. There are lots of terms and important decisions that need to be made at the point where you need to take income. Some of these decisions are not reversible. These decisions are too important to take lightly. Get the best help you can find.

The final source of income to consider will be the assets you have built up in tax-deferred and taxable accounts. These assets are not guaranteed but they are the most common source of retirement income.

SOCIAL SECURITY

Currently, in America, everyone receives Social Security regardless of your level of wealth. Most people consider this system a simple switch that you turn on. It is not a simple switch. There are ways and strategies to maximize your payout. This is especially true if you are divorced, or one spouse earned a lot more income, or your are in great heath and longevity in your genes.

When it comes to planning for any Social Security benefits, there's one factor that is more important than just about anything else, it is your full retirement age (FRA). Many of the benefits you are eligible for are calculated based on how long before or after your FRA they are received. Some of the more advanced Social Security claiming strategies can only be used at FRA or later.

Your FRA has nothing to do with when you actually retire. It is determined solely by when you were born.
Depending on your date of birth, your full retirement age may be anywhere between 65 and 67. You can search online for the chart to determine your FRA based on your DOB.

You can start collecting Social Security retirement benefits as early as age 62. There is a penalty for starting before your full retirement age if you are working. If you receive benefits during a year when you have more than $15, 720 of earned income, you will have $1 of Social Security benefits deducted for every $2 of earned income.   If you have earned income over $41,880, then you will have $1 of Social Security benefits deducted for every $3 of earned income you have over the limit.

This is very confusing and makes it seem like a bad idea to keep working and collect Social Security. I am not sure of the motivation of the people writing these rules but let's keep things simple. (and not conspiratorial). If you're still working before your full retirement age, it usually doesn't pay to start Social Security. This arrangement makes it confusing at best to figure out what is financially appropriate.

From my perspective, it is sad that the government creates rules that discourages young people (those aged 62 to 70) from working. Let me remind you, that if you make it into your 60's, your life expectancy is late eighties or early nineties ... depending on your gender and marital status. That's a 20 to 30 year period. Lots of useful work can still be accomplished. It is sad that the government is encouraging young, competent, brilliant people to retire and stop contributing to society. (or at least stop taking an income)

The point of this book is to live in financial freedom and do the work you enjoy with people you like. That might include getting paid. (ok, I'll get off my soapbox)

If you have stopped working, should you start Social Security at age 62? Maybe. It might make sense for one or both of these reasons.

- You need the money. With little or no earned income and a shortage of other resources, you might have to start Social Security for cash to pay your bills.
- Your health is not great. By age 62, you might have developed a serious medical condition. Taking the money as soon as possible can make sense.

If you don't start Social Security at age 62, you can start any time after that. The waiting game ends at age 70.

Why should you wait? From age 62 to age 70, your monthly check goes up every month you practice patience. When all the numbers are crunched, the annual increase is about 8% a year. That's 8% a year, guaranteed by the feds for the rest of your life.

Some people approach the start-versus-wait decision by looking at the break-even calculation. You might say, how long will I have to live for the amounts added to my monthly checks to catch up with the money I didn't receive while I waited?

That's one way to make the decision.

Another way is to look at waiting as a means of buying "longevity insurance". This provides protection against running out of money in very old age. Today, many people are living into their late 80s, and 90s, and even hitting triple digits. That means a 25 or 30 year retirement. The real risk is running out of money. The fatter Social Security check can really help in those later years.

Our advice is that the higher-earning spouse should generally wait to receive Social Security if they can. When one spouse dies, the survivor will continue to receive the larger of the two spouses' Social Security checks.

IRAs can play a role in your Social Security decision. As you can see, waiting to start as late as possible may payoff. The issue is whether you need more cash flow while you're in your 60's? Conventional wisdom is to delay IRA distributions as long as possible. Required Minimum Distributions (RMDs) start at age 70 ½. The longer you continue tax-deferred building inside an RIA, the more wealth you can accumulate.

Another approach might be to tap the IRA during your 60's and defer the Social Security payout. Each year the Social Security payout increases by 8%. Tax deferral inside an IRA is a real benefit but it might make sense to tap it earlier. This benefit of tax-deferral is most valuable when you are in a high tax bracket. You want to take tax-deferred gains when your tax rate is lowest.

If you expect no real change in your tax rate in your 60's versus your 70's it might make sense to tap the IRA first, let the Social Security payout grow. Then when Social Security starts, you can reduce the amount you are withdrawing from the IRA.

Most people will follow the traditional approach of starting your Social Security in your 60's and begin your IRA deductions in your 70's. Reversing the procedure may be a tax-saver for you. Every situation is different and the IRS rules on withdrawals are complicated. Talk to an expert if you'd like to know if this might be a big win for you.

Under current tax law, IRA distributions are fully taxed. If you withdraw $10,000 from your IRA, you add $10,000 to your taxable income for the year. On the other hand, 85% of Social Security benefits are taxed under current law. If you receive $10,000 from Social Security, no more than $8,500 will be added to your taxable income for the year. Many people include less than 85% of their benefits because they have moderate income, and some report no taxable benefits at all.

Any strategy that substitutes Social Security benefits for IRA withdrawals will be a tax-saver. If overall tax rates rise in the future, as many people expect, this retirement income strategy to become even more tax-efficient.

Keep in mind that Roth IRA distributions are not taxable income. They don't count at all in the formula for taxing your Social Security.

For example, if Carl and Patsy have $30,000 of Roth IRA distributions a year plus $40,000 from Social Security (and no other income). This couple would owe no tax on their Social Security benefits, under the current formula. Roth IRA distributions are tax-free for taxpayers who are at least 59 ½ and have held the accounts at least five years.

This is another reason to build up the Roth IRA for later use.

As you can see, the decision of when to start Social Security is more complicated than just flipping the switch. The decision involves maximizing your potential benefit, saving taxes, and never running out of money.

This section on Social Security is very brief but I hope that I have opened your eyes to some of the possibilities in this area.

PENSIONS

A pension plan is a retirement plan that requires the employer to make contributions into a fund set aside for a worker's future benefit. The employer can be a business, a government, or a union. The pool of funds is invested on the employee's behalf, and the earnings on the investments generate income to the worker upon retirement.

Most businesses have converted their traditional pension plans into 401k plans. Public entities like state and local governments, teachers and nurses unions all still have pension plans. Traditional pension plans are becoming less common. With the advent of 401k plans, employees became responsible for their retirement. In the past, the company or government was responsible for the employee's retirement. This change, which started with the 401k plan in the early eighties, has been a significant culture change in America over the last 30 years.

The thing people like about pension plans is there are no decisions to make other than to show up for work. With at 401k plan or an IRA, there are all these decisions you need to make. A pension is taken care of by the employer. The employer hires a firm to make all of the investment decisions.

The downside to a pension is that if you leave your job you can't take your pension with you. If you receive retirement income depends on how long you were in your job and the employer's vesting schedule. The vesting schedule will vary plan by plan. When you reach retirement age, you will need to reconnect with the firm that runs the company pension plan.

Some people even forget about these pension benefits they have earned. It can come as a nice surprise to remember and reconnect when you start thinking about retirement income. Even a small amount can go a long ways to building a nice retirement income. It all adds up.

Pension income can be a nice piece of the retirement income puzzle. Unfortunately, this type of income is becoming less and less common. On one hand it is nice to have this income but you don't want too much of your income coming from a source like a pension. Any change in the company or government that reduces your benefits can have a devastating effect. It is best to have mulitple sources of income, if possible.

IRAs, 401k, and other tax deferred accounts

A tax deferred account means that your investment earnings like interest, dividends and capital gains grow tax free. The tax free status lasts until you withdraw the funds. The rules for withdrawing money varies depending on the type of tax deferred account.

The most common types of tax deferred accounts are Individual Retirement Accounts (IRA), retirement plan accounts like 401k, or 403b or 457. Taxes can also be deferred inside an annuity.

The benefits of a tax deferred account is that your investments can grow before they are taxed. Taxes are paid at a later date. Another benefits is that, maybe, your tax rate will be lower at the time you need to take the money out of the tax deferred account. This is a big maybe! As we have discussed, the future is uncertain and one uncertainty will be tax rates. What will taxes be in the future? Not idea but we can plan and look for strategies to minimize this impact.

Many people don't realize all the tax deferred account types. We have discussed the 401k account. A 401k is related to a company retirement plan.

A **403(b)** plan, also known as a tax-sheltered annuity (TSA) plan, is a retirement plan for certain employees of public schools, employees of certain tax-exempt organizations, and certain ministers.

A 457 plan is a **defined contribution retirement plan** available to state and local public employees, but can also be offered by certain nonprofit organizations. A 457 plan works much the same way as **401(k) plans**: you can opt to divert part of your salary into the plan, and the money is automatically deducted from your paycheck before taxes are taken out. The money grows tax-deferred until it's withdrawn.

The most common type of tax deferred account is the IRA, Individual Retirement Account. There are various types of IRAs.

1.   Traditional IRA

2.   Roth IRA
     A Roth IRA is for contributions of after tax dollars. When money is withdrawn it is not taxed (because is was taxed before going in). This is an exceptional retirement planning tool. It is important for asset accumulation, income planning, and tax efficiency.

3.   Simplified Employee Pension, or SEP-IRA
     A SEP is a retirement plan for self-employed or small business owners. The key benefit of a SEP over a traditional IRA is the contribution limit. It is much higher than a Traditional IRA.

4.   Savings Incentive Matching for Employers IRA, or SIMPLE IRA
     A SIMPLE IRA is a low-cost way for employers to create a retirement plan without having to setup a 401k plan. This is a great way for a small company to offer a retirement plan benefit to their employees.

5.   Spousal IRA
     To contribute to a Traditional IRA you need earned income. A spousal IRA relaxes that requirement and gives a spouse with low or no annual wages a way to save tax-efficiently for the future. It basically increases the amount a couple can contribute to

Traditional or Roth IRA accounts.

6. Inherited IRA
   An inherited IRA comes from somone who names you as the benefiicary on their IRA account. This is not a spouse because that is handled differently. It usually comes from a parent or friend. There are rules about how to take the distribution of an inherited IRA. Please talk to someone who knows about this. People lose thousands and thousands of dollars by not doing this correctly.

Most people don't realize how many different variations of the traditional IRA are in use. Each of these variations have different rules. That is why it is imperitive you know the rules. The definitive source for up to date rules is the IRS. They publish a document every year with all the new changes. (because the rules change every year, if not sooner)

The rulebook for this is called Publication 590, Individual Retirement Arrangements (IRAs). It has recently been split into two documents. They are:

> Publication 590-A. Contributions to Individual Retirement Arrangement (IRAs)
> Publication 590-B. Distributions from Individuals Retirement Arrangement (IRAs)

Just Google this for detail. We strongly recommend professional help in this area. The rules are complex and a mistake is costly. Make sure you find good advice.

Most retirement assets are in tax-deferred accounts. There are a couple ideas to keep in mind regarding these accounts. We are not going to discuss specific rules because they change on a regular basis.

1. **When do I have to withdraw the money and pay the tax?**
   Many times people don't consider that, at some point, the government wants their "fair share" of taxes. (whatever that is) For most tax-deferred accounts that age is 70 ½ years old. I know 70 ½. Leave it to the government to make it complicated. Rules can vary by account type.

2. **Is there a penalty for withdrawing my money early (before the government rules say is appropriate)?**
Most penalities apply before age 59 ½. The penalty is 10%. An remember you will pay the tax as well. So it will be tax rate plus 10%. This varies as well. A 457 acount does not have this rule.

We are going to talk a lot more about tax saving strategies in the tax planning section. You may be starting to realize the impact of taxes on your income plan. A big part of retirement income planning is understanding tax laws and making sure you are doing the right thing. Qualified help is a big deal.

ANNUITIES

We discussed annuities in the section on investments. As you may recall, annuities can be used as an alternative to cash. They are an important investment component but they are also part of the income planning step. Annuities have the option to be converted to an income stream. The process of converting a deferred annuity into an immediate annuity is called annuitization.

Annuitization is the process of converting an annuity investment into a series of periodic income payments. Annuities may be annuitized for a specific period of time or for the life of the annuitant. This is an important decision. Ask for help and a second opinion concerning making this decision.

Keep in mind that before you annuitize, the money belongs to you. This means that you can move the money to another insurance company that may be competing for your business. Or you may want to move the money if the company has financial difficulty. Remember that conditions change and there may be better options for this money.

After you annuitize, the insurance company owns the money. You have traded the money for a guarantee. The guarantee will be for an income stream for life. This is why this decision is so important. It really locks you in to that specific insurance company after you make the decision.

Annuities can be considered private or personal pensions. They can be built by individutals. This process of annuitization converts your assets into a guaranteed stream of income just like a pension from a government or a company. Pretty cool!.

When you add your Social Security payments, pension (if you are one of the lucky few) and investment income, there may be a gap in your primary income need. One solution may be to use some of your assets to purchase an annuity with a lifetime income rider. This may cover the gap and protect against longevity. The income stream may also be adjusted for inflation if desired. This is a complicated planning question. Be very careful about this decision. There are powerful companies that would love to tie up your money in their program. Consult an independent professional before making this decision.

Taxable Accounts

The last bucket of money to consider for retirement income is taxable accounts. This is any money you have paid tax on and saved. This is the money you have in banks, at brokers, or directly in mutual funds. It will include individual or joint investment accounts. Sometimes these are called brokerage accounts.

When you hear about saving and investing for retirement, most think of tax-deferred accounts like we have discussed above. These accounts offer excellent tax advantages, but that doesn't mean investors should overlook the benefits associated with taxable accounts.

IRAs and 401k accounts enjoy tax-deferred growth but they come with lots of rules and restrictions. We recommend investment accounts like this because they offer key benefits. The benefits include: flexibility, more control when you start taking income, ability to minimize taxes, no required minimum distribution, ability to transfer to your heirs with fewer limitations.

If you are maximizing your taxes by the use of tax-deferred accounts, the next step will be to create a taxable account to build assets and save money.

Let's now turn our attention to reasonalbe withdrawal rate. Fun stuff!

STEP 3:
Start With A Reasonable Withdrawal Rate, And Be Prepared To Change It.

Once you determine out how much your retirement expenses will be, the big question then becomes how much can you afford to withdraw each year without running too big a risk of outliving your savings?

Traditionally, many retirees relied on the 4% rule, which essentially holds that if you limit your initial draw to 4% of your savings and then adjust for inflation each year, there's a high probability that your savings will last at least 30 years. Given the low investment returns projected for the years ahead, however, some retirement experts believe that an initial withdrawal rate of 3% makes more sense.

Whatever withdrawal rate you start with be prepared to raise or lower withdrawals in subsequent years. Anywhere between 3% and 4% is reasonable for a 30-year-plus time horizon. These assumptions may need to change based on market conditions and how much you actually spend.

For example, if your account balance dips due to a market setback you may need to make adjustments. If unexpected expense forces you to pull more from your retirement accounts than you planned, then you may need to scale back withdrawals. This may last for only a few years so that your nest egg has a chance to recover.

On the other hand, if a string of outsize market gains boosts the value of your retirement accounts, you may be able to spend more freely for a few years. These types of adjustments are crucial to your success.

There are plenty of other ways you can refine and improve your retirement income strategy. They might include doing some lifestyle planning to get a better sense of how you'll actually live once you retire. Another thing to do give your portfolio a check-up to make sure it's properly positioned for retirement.

Keep in mind that professional financial planners have very sophisticated software tools to do a lot of this work for you. You must do the work to initiate the process, talk to the planner and engage in the process. But there are extremely qualified people available to help you.

All of this will help. But you will need to take action on these three steps. If you do you can be reasonably confident that you'll have the retirement income you need for as long as you'll need. Keep in mind that income planning is not a do it and be done project. This is an ongoing project.

Important questions to answer

1. How much will I need to live on each year?
2. What sources will fund this amount?
3. Which assets should I turn to first if I'm at least age 59 ½?
4. How can I increase investment income?
5. How much emergency cash should I set aside?
6. What debts should I pay off before retirement?
7. Should I roll my 401k into my IRA?
8. Should I convert all or part of my Traditional IRA into a Roth IRA?
9. How can I make sure my life insurance policy is on schedule to pay off?
10. Do I need long-term care insurance?

"The best we can do is size up the chances, calculate the risks involved, estimate our ability to deal with them, and then make our plans with confidence." — Henry Ford

SECTION 3:

Insurance

Insurance is risk management and an important step in financial planning. Insurance is the process of transferring the risk of potential loss to someone else, usually an insurance company. The price to transfer that risk is called a premium.

Your need for insurance changes with your stage of life and level of wealth. When you are young with children, life insurance is vital. When you are older and wealthy, an umbrella policy might be appropriate to protect from lawsuits. The key in this area is knowing your risks and protecting appropriately.

Insurance allows you to protect yourself against significant potential loss and financial hardship at an affordable rate. Everyone has needs to protect themselves or someone else against financial hardship. These types of risk may include:

- Protecting family after one's death from loss of income

- Ensuring debt repayment after death

- Protecting against the death of a key employee or person in your business

- Protecting your business from business interruption and loss of income

- Protecting yourself against unforeseeable health expenses

- Protecting your home against theft, fire, flood and other hazards

- Protecting yourself against lawsuits

- Protecting yourself in the event of disability

- Protecting your car against theft or losses incurred because of accidents

- And many more

Insurance is an extensive field. For complex cases, I will work with a person with focused expertise in a specific area of insurance. The field of insurance is large and varied. My best advice is to determine the expertise you need and find the person with the extensive experience in that area.

When it comes to insurance, I know the field from years of experience but I don't pretend to be an expert. I hope that I know when I don't know what I'm talking about in this area. Part of my work is building relationships with people in the field so that when my clients need deep expertise, we can find the right person quickly and build a team to solve a problem.

We all hear about how schools don't educate our children about finances, insurance is even further down the list of topics that are covered. Insurance is actually an interesting idea of how to spread risks among a large group of people so that everyone receives a benefit. Insurance is definitely an adult topic that we must face.

Here is a list of the types of insurance that you may need to consider.

- **Life insurance**. Generally, people buy a life insurance policy after they're married or have a child. The thinking behind life insurance is that if your death would create a financial hardship for those you leave behind, then you need life insurance. Many discussions we have with older clients is whether to keep their life policies after their kids are grown. There are many details that go into this decision. Life insurance is necessary depending on who is depending on you. Not everyone needs a life insurance policy but it's important to know for sure if you do

- **Homeowners insurance.** If you own a house, your bank will require you to have homeowners insurance. If someone loses their homeowners insurance for some reason – cancellation, nonpayment, nonrenewal, then the bank is notified. The bank will immediately place their own insurance on the property and send the bill to you. The bank will not allow it to go uninsured for any length of time. If your mortgage is paid off, you can make the choice to not have your home covered by insurance. Not a good bet in case of fire or worse.

- **Auto insurance.** This is another must-have. In fact, it's against the law to drive without some sort of coverage. If you're caught driving without insurance, you probably won't go to jail, but your driver's license will likely be suspended and you'll be fined.

- **Medical &Health insurance.** This is a must-have and there is a lot to know and consider in this section. If you work for a company that has health care coverage, that is great. If not, there are lots of things to consider. Find someone what deals with health care coverage every day. They will be a big help.

- **Disability insurance**. If you are working for a company, most will offer some level of disability insurance. If you are self-employed, you need to consider covering this for yourself. Disability insurance replaces your income if we become incapacitated and can't work. This is very important when a household depends on you and your income. Find an expert.

- **Umbrella insurance.** This is important to consider as your wealth grows. Think of this as insurance for your insurance. It's an extra amount of liability coverage in $1 million increments that protects over and above your personal and auto liabilities. If you are in an auto accident, it is possible that the policy pays and there is still personal liability for injuries. This liability falls to you and the assets you own. For those in the upper middle class and higher should consider umbrella insurance. A family can add this policy for between $250 to $300 a year.

There are other types of insurance but these are the primary types to consider. There are many other types for smaller risks.

More details on Life Insurance

When it comes to life insurance, the policies offered can contain a lot of bells and whistles. This can be helpful but it adds lots of confusion about what is really important.

Term life insurance is the most basic type of life insurance policy. You pay a relatively low annual premium for coverage that remains in force for a specific number of years (the term) – provided the premiums are paid. You can buy a "level term" policy in which the premium stays the same annually for the duration of the policy. Or you can buy annual renewable term, in which the premium starts out very low but inches up annually over the policy's term. This is the first step to having life insurance.

If you have kids and no other life insurance, this is the place to start. The cost of term insurance is usually very reasonable. Permanent life insurance is where things get a little more complex.

Permanent insurance provides lifelong protection, and the ability to accumulate cash value on a tax-deferred basis. Unlike term **insurance**, a **permanent insurance** policy will remain in force for as long as you continue to pay your premiums.

The need for life insurance can persist after the kids have graduated college or the mortgage has been paid off. If you died the day after your youngest child graduated from college, your spouse would still be faced with daily living expenses. Would your financial plan, without life insurance, enable your spouse to maintain the lifestyle you worked so hard to achieve? These are big questions and one reason for permanent insurance.

A key characteristic of permanent insurance is a feature known as cash value or cash-surrender value. Permanent insurance is often referred to as cash-value insurance because these types of policies can build cash value over time, as well as provide a death benefit to your beneficiaries.

"Permanent insurance" is really a catchall phrase for a wide variety of life insurance products that contain the cash-value feature. Within this class of life insurance, there are a multitude of different products. Here we list the most common ones.

Whole Life or Ordinary Life

If you're the kind of person who likes predictability over time, Whole Life insurance might be right for you. It provides you with the certainty of a guaranteed amount of death benefit and a guaranteed rate of return on your cash values. And you'll have a level premium that is guaranteed to never increase for life.

Another valuable benefit of a participating Whole Life policy is the opportunity to earn dividends. While your policy's guarantees provide you with a minimum death benefit and cash value, dividends give you the opportunity to receive an enhanced death benefit and cash value growth. Dividends, if left in the policy, can provide an offset (and more) to the eroding effects of inflation on your coverage amount.

Variable Life

Variable Life insurance provides death benefits and cash values that vary with the performance of a portfolio of underlying investment options. You can allocate your premiums among a variety of investment options offering different degrees of risk and reward: stocks, bonds, combinations of both, or a fixed account that guarantees interest and principal.

This type of insurance is for people who are willing to assume investment risk to try to achieve greater returns. With Variable Life you're shifting much of the investment risk from the insurance company to yourself. Good investment performance would provide the potential for higher cash values and ultimate death benefits. If the specified investments perform poorly, cash values and death benefits would drop accordingly.

Universal Life

Unlike Whole Life and Variable Life where you pay fixed premiums, Universal Life offers adjustable premiums that give you the option to make higher premium payments when you have extra cash on hand or lower ones when money is tight.

Universal Life allows you, after your initial payment, to pay premiums at any time, in virtually any amount, subject to certain minimums and maximums. You also can reduce or increase the death benefit more easily than under a traditional Whole Life policy.

Most Universal Life policies will also provide a guaranteed rate of return on your cash values, with one important exception. It is possible that you will not accumulate any cash value if any, or all, of the following circumstances occur: administrative expenses increase, mortality assumptions are changed, the insurance company's investment portfolio underperforms, premium payments are insufficient.

Variable Universal Life

Variable Universal Life insurance is a flexible premium, permanent life insurance policy that allows you to have premium dollars allocated to a variety of investment options, offering varying degrees of risk and reward. These policies are a good choice for people seeking maximum flexibility.

Life insurance can be an effective tool for diversification. Some policies can help you reduce risk and protect wealth from the effect of taxes, market volatility and longevity.

As you can see, there are lots of things to consider in the area of insurance. We will stop here but, I hope you realize, how important insurance is to your overall financial plan.

SECTION 4:
Tax Planning

Tax planning permeates the financial planning process. As you may recall, we talked about taxes a lot in the investment and income planning sections. The reason for this attention to tax issues is that taxes are a real drag on your ability to build wealth. And there are ways to reduce your tax burden if you are paying attention. (If you are content to not pay attention, the government is content to take all the taxes they can.)

The purpose of tax planning is to ensure tax efficiency and that you are paying your fair share. Your financial plan should be tuned to reduce your tax liability and maximize your eligibility to contribute to a retirement account. Tax planning is the art of arranging your affairs in ways that postpone or avoid taxes. By employing effective tax planning strategies, you can have more money to save and invest or more money to spend. Or both. Your choice.

Put another way, tax planning means deferring and flat out avoiding taxes by taking advantage of beneficial tax-law provisions, increasing and accelerating tax deductions and tax credits, and generally making maximum use of all applicable breaks available under our beloved Internal Revenue Code.

As an aside, I love the phrase "fair share". Not sure what it really means and that is why politicians use it so much. What is your fair share? The IRS and tax professionals spend all their time discussing, bickering, and fighting over what is a person's "fair share". I share an office with a large public accounting firm and I hear the conversations, frustration and disagreement that happens between US citizens and the tax authorities. It ain't always pretty. The IRS and the state and local tax collector's can have some pretty crazy ideas about what is your fair share. This is why it pays to have representation. If you don't know the rules the tax authorities will definitely take advantage of you.

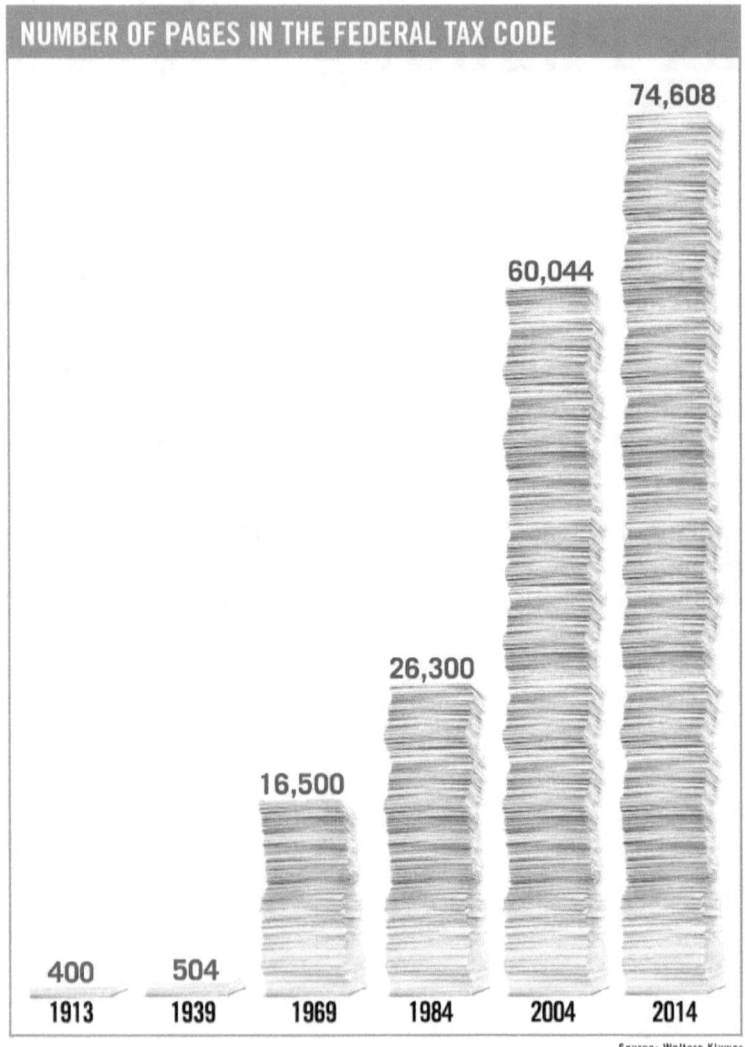

NUMBER OF PAGES IN THE FEDERAL TAX CODE

400	504	16,500	26,300	60,044	74,608
1913	1939	1969	1984	2004	2014

Source: Wolters Kluwer

And with a tax code of 74,608 pages, the Federal tax code has a lot of room for disagreement. When the IRS was created in 1913, the tax code was 400 pages. "Over the decades, lawmakers have increasingly asked the tax code to direct all manner of social and economic objectives, such as encouraging people to buy hybrid vehicles, turn corn into gasoline, purchase health insurance, buy a home, replace that home's windows, adopt children, put them in daycare, purchase school supplies, go to college, invest in historic buildings, spend more on research, and the list goes on," according to the Tax Foundation.

With all this complexity, it is important that you protect yourself. The best way to do that is with knowledge. You can spend the time educating yourself, and I recommend that. But you also should find the best tax professionals you can afford. As the insurance and estate planning, I am not an expert in these fields and so I rely on professionals to direct my clients. Part of my responsibility to my clients is to ensure they are getting the best possible tax advice. The planning process and the tax discussions help me to make this assessment.

Tax planning during the accumulation phase and tax planning during the distribution phase are very different. It's important to understand the differences and be prepared to adjust your strategy accordingly. The accumulation phase is the period when you enter the workforce and begin saving funds for later in your life. The accumulation phase ends, and distribution begins, when you actually retire or start withdrawing funds on a regular basis.

During the accumulation phase, you will be making your payroll contributions to the Social Security system, and you will be contributing to your company 401k plan, if you have one. You may also contribute to your IRAs, either traditional or Roth. It is usually best to maximize your contributions to tax deferred accounts like 401k, 403b, or IRAs.

Your contributions to tax deferred accounts is part of the discussion you need to have with your tax professional. A financial advisor can give you general tax advice, but we cannot give detailed tax advice because we don't always see the tax returns and all the factors going into your tax situation.

Many great questions come up during tax planning. It is a good idea to hold a joint meeting with your financial advisor and your tax person. You don't need to do this every year but you should do it to get the strategies in place and working for you. You can also review your strategies when you have major life events that can change your strategy. Otherwise, they won't change much year to year. (unless of course there are major tax law changes).

When you are working, the tax strategies will vary based on whether you are an employee, self-employed or a business owner. The business owner has the most flexibility and I recommend a CPA or business savvy tax preparer to put the best plan in place. The employee has very limited options when it comes to tax strategy.

In preparation for financial freedom, I recommend that you begin to plan what you really want to do when you are financially free. One part of this journey may be to form a business around the activities you plan to do during your freedom phase. ;) The things you learn, while still working and accumulating assets, will be a great benefit when you achieve your freedom. You will also be able to get familiar with tax strategies that business owners use.

Tax strategy comes down to reducing the current year tax obligation and deferring taxes that must be paid in the future. The current tax year obligation is about reducing your taxable income by taking deductions or writing off expenses first. For employees who are paid on a W2, the options are very limited beyond home interest deduction, charitable contributions, and various other tax credits.

For business owners, the strategies are much more diverse and attractive. We are not going to delve into them here but just know that having a side business can be a very good idea. It will help you learn and understand how to be a better investor and tax strategist.

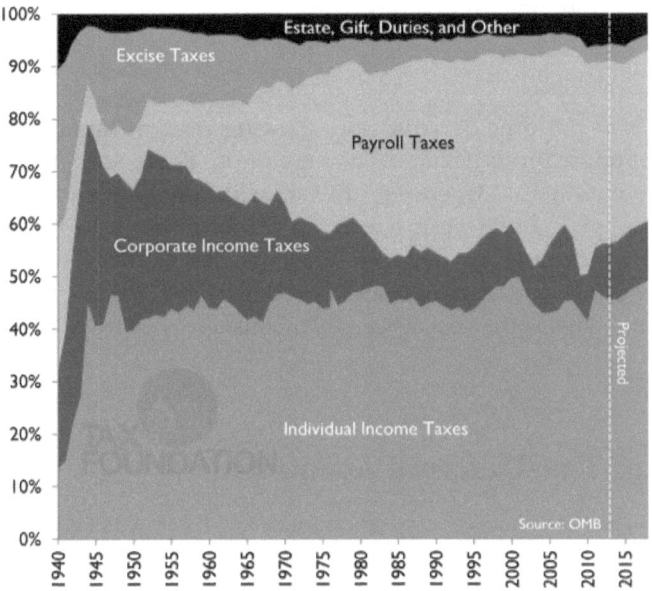

The Composition of Federal Revenues Has Changed Over Time

Estate, Gift, Duties, and Other

Excise Taxes

Payroll Taxes

Corporate Income Taxes

Individual Income Taxes

Source: OMB

Projected

TAX DEFERRED ACCOUNTS

After considering current year tax obligations, our attention turns to deferring taxes until a later date. These tax-deferred accounts typically have penalties for early withdrawal and require that you begin withdrawing money at 70 ½ years old. (don't ask me why 70 ½, it's the government, it does not have to be logical)

The great thing about these accounts is that is motivates you from two perspectives, maybe three. The first is tax deferral and the second is simple savings. It's a one-two punch. And, for some of you, you may have a company match for money contributed to these accounts.

Using tax-deferred investment accounts makes the most sense if you are in a high tax bracket now and think you will be in a lower tax bracket in the future when you will be taking withdrawals. This idea is considered suspect by some because of the expectation of higher taxes for everyone in the future. This may be true and is the argument for the use of the Roth IRA. (more on that in a bit)

The idea is to put time on your side, allowing years of investment income to compound, without having to pay tax on it. These accounts have been a great invention for Americans. But as with anything successful, it has become complex. Every year, books are written about how to manage and strategize concerning tax-deferred accounts. As we have discussed, it is possible to cost yourself thousands of dollars by making mistakes with your money. This is the area where many mistakes occur.

Types of Tax-Deferred Accounts

Below is a list of the types of accounts that have a tax-deferred status. Inside of these accounts you can own just about any type of investment you can think of; mutual funds, stocks, bonds, certificates of deposit, fixed annuities, variable annuities, real estate, etc.

- **Traditional IRAs -** investments inside of a traditional IRA grow tax-deferred. Your contributions to a traditional IRA may also be tax deductible if you meet the IRA contribution limits and rules requirements.

- **Retirement plans like 401(k) accounts, 403(b) plans and 457 plans -** investments inside of employer-sponsored retirement plans usually grow tax deferred until such time as you take withdrawals. Contributions may also be tax deductible. When you change employers you can avoid a taxable withdrawal by using an IRA rollover to move funds directly from your plan to an IRA account, or by moving the funds directly to a plan with your new employer.

- **Roth IRAs -** investments inside of a Roth IRA are even better than tax-deferred; they grow tax-free as long as you follow the Roth IRA withdrawal rules.

You can accumulate tax-deferred savings in several ways:

1. Fund tax-deferred accounts like an IRA or employer-sponsored retirement plan (such as a 401(k), 457 or 403(b) plan).

2. Put money in a tax-deferred annuity which is an insurance contract that allows you to accumulate tax-deferred savings. Tax-deferred annuities can be fixed, which offer a guaranteed rate, or variable, where it allows you to choose from a variety of investments.

3. Accumulate money inside a whole life insurance policy, or fund Roth IRAs, Health Savings Accounts, or by using certain types of government bonds such as Series EE Bonds or I-Bonds.

Example of How Tax-Deferral Works

- You invest $1,000 in a tax-deferred savings account (like a 401(k) plan, or IRA account), or use a tax-deferred annuity.

- It earns 5% in investment income.

- At the end of the year, the investment is worth $1,050.

- You do *not* have to claim the $50 as investment income on your current year's tax return since it was earned inside of a tax-deferred account or tax-deferred annuity.

- Next year, the original $1,000 and the $50 of interest are both earning more interest for you.

Early Withdrawals

When you use accounts that allow you to defer taxes until later, withdrawals of investment gain prior to age 59 ½ are usually subject to a 10% penalty tax. This penalty is in addition to ordinary income taxes. Think of it like this: the IRS allows you to grow your funds tax-deferred as an incentive to encourage you to save for retirement, but they penalize you if you use the funds too early. Not all types of tax-deferred options have an early withdrawal penalty. Consult a professional.

When Do I Pay Taxes?

At the time that you take a withdrawal from a tax-deferred savings account, you will pay taxes at your ordinary income tax rate on any investment gain that is withdrawn. If your contributions to the account were also tax deductible then you will pay taxes on the full amount of your withdrawal, not just the investment gain portion. These withdrawals are known as RMDs, or Required Minimum Distributions. Consult a professional because a mistake in this area will cost you a 50% penalty. (that is not a typo ... 50% penalty)

There are thousands of rules and hundreds of strategies to get the most benefit from these tax-deferred accounts. This area is really important to work with people that know what they are doing. A mistake here can cost you thousands of dollars. I've seen it, and it ain't pretty.

After you stop working, you'll need cash for living expenses. Here's a simple suggested sequence for withdrawing cash from the various account types. Some combination of withdrawals across different types of accounts often produces the most tax-efficient results.

1. Start with your taxable accounts. In these low-yield times, investment interest and dividends alone probably won't pay your bills. You'll need to take withdrawals and sell assets. Fortunately, taxes on these transactions like to be the lowest.
2. Move money from tax-deferred accounts such as Traditional IRAs and 401ks to your Roth IRA. Again, these will be taxable transactions but you may not owe much in tax if you are not working and you are in a lower tax bracket. Pay any tax from your taxable accounts.
3. Draw down your tax-deferred accounts. Once you've depleted your taxable accounts. Either use the money for spending or move money into your Roth IRA.
4. Try to wait until age 70 to start Social Security benefits. Among married couples, it often makes sense for one spouse to start at full retirement age (66 or 67) while the other delays until 70. Ideally, getting into your 70s with maximum Social Security

benefits and all your savings in Roth accounts will put you in a great position for many years to come. Your Social Security benefits will be untaxed or lightly taxed, under current law, and Roth distributions won't be taxed. Roth IRAs have no Required Minimum Distributions so money you don't need can pass to your beneficiaries, for ongoing tax free accumulation and distribution.

Many people will ask, why bother saving in an IRA? If you're contributing to a 401k at work, you may be wondering why you need a Individual Retirement Account (IRA). Or you may feel you can't afford to save the max in both. But opening and saving even a little in a IRA is important. Here's why …

1) Tax-free growth. Assets in an IRA grow tax-free- meaning there are no taxes on capital gains when you sell assets within the account. Taxes are paid at distribution.
2) Tax deduction. You can always deduct your full contribution.
3) Investment freedom. Unlike a 401k, which offers a limited selection of investments, and IRA lets you invest in any asset you wish.

Many people don't save and invest because they don't feel they have flexibility in their budgets. They don't think a little bit will matter. Consider this, if you make $36,000 a year in income. That is $3000 a month. One percent of $3000 is $30. Are you really gonna tell me that you can't afford to save $30 a month?   1% is a starting point. For many people, they just need to get started.

TAXABLE ACCOUNTS

The tax strategy for a taxable account is completely different from a tax-deferred account. For taxable accounts, investors must pay taxes on their investment income in the year it was received. This difference has implications for the type of investments you put into these accounts and the strategies for trading and investing.

A taxable account is a bank account, or an investment account, or a money market account. It is any account that does not a tax-deferred.

There are tax rules regarding these accounts, but the rules are not as extensive as a tax-deferred account.

For whatever reason, we hear it time and again to invest in a 401k or an IRA or a Roth IRA. This is sound advice but the taxable account does not get the respect it deserves. There are many benefits to having a taxable investment account and this should not be overlooked by investors.

After you have invested all that you can in your employer-sponsored retirement plan. And you have maxed out your IRA options, too. You will need to invest more to reach your goals. You need to set up a taxable account. We have talked about cash reserves and when you maximize you tax-deferred benefits continue to save in these accounts.

The benefits of taxable accounts are their flexibility, opportunity for tax efficiency, no required minimum distributions, tax savings for heirs and tax loss harvesting. When my clients have established the maximum deferrals allowed and save 3 to 6 months of cash reserves, we establish a taxable account to save and grow their wealth. It is very exciting for me when a client gets to this level of saving and investing. Great and exciting things start to happen.

Which investments are better for taxable accounts? Stocks and **stock funds** - because they generate lower taxes than taxable bonds and bond funds do. Municipal bonds, which generate tax-free income, are also better off in regular investment accounts.

But even within the stock portion of your portfolio, there are differences that may affect your strategy of what to put where. The most tax-efficient - that is, the lowest-taxed - stock investments are individual stocks that you buy and hold, rather than actively trade. That's because you get taxed on the dividends (if any) every year, but you don't get taxed on the capital gains until you sell.

The second most tax-efficient kind of stock investment is a stock index fund or stock index ETF. That's because index funds trade stocks relatively infrequently, racking up fewer "realized gains" than actively managed funds do.

The least tax-efficient kind of stock investment is an actively managed stock fund. So let's say that you've already put all your bonds and bond funds in your **401(k)** and **IRA**, and still have room to put some stocks or stock funds there. If you have any actively managed stock funds, move them there first.

This type of allocation is vital to your investment success. And if you don't know the rules and strategies it will really cost you. (And you may not even realize it.)

As you can see, there are many tax issues to consider. Many more tax issues than we can consider in this section. We are not going to address Medicare in this book either but it is an important planning topic to discuss with your financial advisor.

Any way you slice it, taxes are a drain on your investment performance. Whether you know the effect of this or not, it is affecting your livelihood. Taxes are a vital component to consider in any successful investment strategy.

The definitive rule book for all of these tax account questions is the IRS Publication 590, Individual Retirement Arrangements (IRAs). It has now grown and split into two publications. It is now:

- Publication 590-A. Contributions to Individual Retirement Arrangement (IRAs)
- Publication 590-B. Distributions from Individuals Retirement Arrangement (IRAs)

Let's move on.

"It's the little details that are vital. Little things make big things happen." – John Wooden

SECTION 5:
Estate Planning

Estate planning is the final pillar to your complete financial plan. To put it simply, estate planning involves deciding how you want your assets distributed after you die (or become unable to make your own financial decisions). Estate planning can be complicated and emotional, so it is best to consult an estate attorney and include your financial advisor.

Believe it or not, you have an estate. An estate is everything that you own: your bank accounts, your investment accounts, your home, your car, real estate and other property, life insurance, furniture, and any smaller assets you have in your name. Everyone has an estate. Some estates are bigger than others and therefore planning is required based on the assets you own. Your estate might include things like a song you wrote or even a social media account.

An estate plan will include instructions on how your assets will be gifted to your heirs. It will give you control over how things are given to the people and organizations you care most about. To ensure your wishes are carried out, you need to provide instructions on **who** you want to receive **what** and **when** (usually upon your death). You want all of this done with the least amount paid in taxes, legal fees, and court costs.

That is estate planning – making a plan in advance and naming whom you want to receive the things you own after you die. A good estate plan can include several elements:

A last will and testament lets you choose who inherits your assets, select guardians for your children, and name an executor to make sure your wishes are carried out.

A power of attorney gives the person you name the authority to manage your financial affairs if you are unable to do so. They are empowered to do things like pay your bills and access your accounts if you are not able to do so.

A living will is a statement of your wishes for the kind of life-sustaining medical intervention you want, or don't want, in the event that you become terminally ill and unable to communicate.

A healthcare power of attorney authorizes someone you trust to make medical decisions on your behalf. This is usually a spouse, family member or close friend.

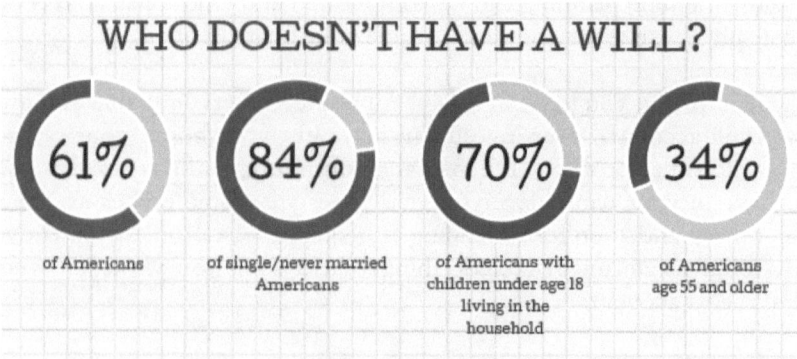

WHO DOESN'T HAVE A WILL?

61%
of Americans

84%
of single/never married Americans

70%
of Americans with children under age 18 living in the household

34%
of Americans age 55 and older

For some people, a **trust** may also make sense. A trust is a legal entity that lets you put conditions on how certain assets are distributed upon your death. A trust can also be a part of your tax strategy to minimize gift and estate taxes. The accounts that have been put into a trust bypass probate, which can be a long drawn out process.

Please note that creating a trust is only the first step in protecting your assets from the probate process. The second step is to re-title the accounts and property into the trust. You'd be surprised how many people have a trust created but do not move assets into the trust. Some attorneys will handle this process for you (and some will not). A trust with no assets in it is useless.

There are two basic types of trusts: living trust and testamentary trusts. A living trust is set up during someone's lifetime. A testamentary trust is set up in a will and only goes into effect after death.

Living trusts can be revocable and irrevocable. Revocable trusts allow you to retain control of all the assets in the trust, and you are free to revoke or change the terms at any time. In an irrevocable trust, the assets placed in the trust are no longer yours. You can't make changes to the trust without the beneficiary's consent. The assets in the trust are not subject to estate taxes.

There are other types of trusts that are more complicated but these trusts are designed for specific situations. We are not going to address those here.

Most estates -- more than 99.7% -- will not owe federal estate taxes. For someone who dies in 2016, the federal government will impose estate tax only if your taxable estate is worth more than $5.45 million. (This exemption amount rises each year to adjust for inflation.) Married couples estate tax exemption is doubled. All the assets left to a spouse (as long as the spouse is a U.S. citizen) or tax-exempt.

Do I need an estate plan?

This area of financial planning can be neglected because it is sometimes hard to address uncomfortable questions like, "What happens to my assets when I die?" It is hard to address the questions of "who will get what when I die" and "who will be in charge"?

Most people with assets or a family should execute a will. However, not everyone needs an estate plan. The decision is a personal one and depends on the complexity and size of your assets. Consider the following questions:

1. Are there children involved?

2. Who would you want to name as guardian and inheritance manager for your minor children?

3. How large is the estate, and which state is it in?

4. If you have any type of retirement account, such as a 401(k), 403(b), IRA, or Roth IRA, can its distribution to the beneficiaries be "stretched"?

5. Is privacy important?

6. Would you like some money to go to charities?

7. If you own a business, have you thought about succession planning?

8. What life stage are you in? Is estate planning becoming more important?

9. What are your instructions for your care if you become disabled before you die?

10. Are there members of your family who might be irresponsible with money and may need protection from creditors or divorce?

11. Are there special circumstances to consider (like blended families or disabilities)?

Even if your assets are below the level of the estate tax, consider how your family will distribute your assets when you die. If you are married, your spouse will get everything you own (unless special instructions are established). If you are not married, and have several children it can be a real mess for them to figure out who gets what. Do your family a favor, get a will at least, and save them the trouble of dealing with this.

You want to avoid probate court because of the cost and because you are putting decisions in the hands of a judge and court system that will not understand your wishes (unless they are spelled out). The role of the probate court judge is to assure that the deceased debts are paid and that any remaining assets are distributed to the proper beneficiaries. It will help your family if you outline your wishes ahead of time.

Unlike a will, a trust does not die when you die. Assets can stay in the trust, managed by the trustee you select, until your wishes are fulfilled. This timeframe can be controlled by the age of your beneficiaries, or the capacity of the beneficiaries. There may be special needs to consider, may be to protect assets from beneficiaries creditors, spouses and irresponsible spending.

One important thing to do, even if you don't have a trust or will, is to ensure that the beneficiaries are setup properly. Some accounts or assets can't have beneficiaries assigned. Real estate or a bank account can't have a beneficiary assigned. A tax-deferred account like an IRA, or 401k, or life insurance policy can have a beneficiary assigned. Some types of investment accounts can be setup with a beneficiary, if you investment advisor knows what they are doing. Check with your advisor on this.

If you have assets listed in your last will, you are on the right track, but a last will still has to go through probate court. The way to avoid probate court is with the use of the revocable or irrevocable trust. This will allow you to transfer ownership of all assets exactly as you wish should you become incapacitated or pass away.

It is important to review these documents on a regular basis. One of the routine things we do with clients is to review beneficiary forms. It is very common for people to have kids and they not be listed as a beneficiary. This is important if something should happen to you and your spouse, you want the money to go directly to your kids and avoid the court.

It is also important to review beneficiaries for other life changes. It is more common than you think for someone to die and their IRA goes to their x-wife. Talk about unhappy people, this makes people pretty unhappy.

Your estate plan should be dynamic, not a once-and-done document. Your plan needs to keep pace with your life changes. It needs to adjust to changes in the accumulation of wealth and changes in family structure. Expect your plan to look different at 80 years old than it will look when you are 40.

If you have children, a will can give the parent the opportunity to name a guardian if something should happen to them. In addition to guardian, who assumes responsibility for the care and custody of a minor child? If the child is inheriting assets, who will be in charge of these assets until they become an adult. A will can give you the opportunity to outline your wishes in this area.

Estate planning is for everyone. It is not just for "the wealthy". Good estate planning often means more for families with modest assets, because they have the least to lose. Many will put off estate planning because they believe they don't own enough, they're not old enough, they're busy, or they're confused and don't know who can help them. If you don't have a plan, your state has one for you, but you probably won't like it.

Plus the burden on your family is big enough with your absence. Given a choice wouldn't you want matters to be handled by your family, and not by the courts.

Get organized and be prepared!

Estate planning does not have to be expensive. A big part of it is having your records in order so that someone can find them easily. Would your family know where to find your financial records, titles, insurance policies if something happened to you?

For my clients, I recommend a big binder with pockets. Make copies of documents and keep bank statements and investment statements current, at least annually. When your family visits, show them the binder on the shelf and tell them, check here is anything happens to me.

This is a big help to your family. I cannot tell you how many calls I have gotten over the years from family members looking for a copy of the trust or will. We do not typically have these documents but you can hear the desperation in their voices. They know mom or dad had a trust but they just can't find it. So sad!

Here is some of the pertinent information to include in the binder.

1. Drivers License, Passport, Social Security card, Medicare card and Medicare supplemental insurance card. Make a copy of these and include in your binder.
2. Doctors names and contact information
3. Birth certificate
4. Marriage license
5. Legal documents like powers of attorney for finances, advance directive, trust and will
6. Current bank statements, at least annually update.
7. Current investment statements, at least annually update.
8. Current 1099's
9. Current W-2's
10. Current income tax return
11. Current property tax statement
12. Grant deed to any property
13. Veteran's discharge papers (DD-214)
14. Account and/or computer passwords

Many times when a family is looking for documents when someone passes, they don't even know what they are looking for. They may not know about a life insurance policy, or a savings account. A binder like this, even if it is out of date, can help your family tremendously.

The best time is now!

If you don't think you can afford a complex estate plan now, start with what you *can* afford. For a young family or single adult, that may mean a will, term life insurance, and powers of attorney for your assets and health care decisions. Then, let your planning develop and expand as your needs change and your financial situation improves. An experienced attorney will be able to provide critical guidance and peace of mind that your documents are prepared properly.

Don't wait! You can put something in place now and change it later, which is exactly the way estate planning should be done. And the best benefit will be achieved, which is peace of mind. This is one of the most thoughtful and considerate things you can do for yourself and for those you love.

PART 3:

The Freedom

In our house there is a rite of passage that involves watching a movie. We have four boys and they are ten years apart in age, the oldest to the youngest. We just recently held the rite of passage event with our two younger boys. They are teenagers now and are becoming men. If you are a parent, you know what an interesting process it is to watch your children grow up. You want to instill in them important lessons that hopefully they will carry with them throughout life.

The movie that we watch together is Braveheart. Braveheart is a 1995 epic directed by and starring Mel Gibson. The story is about William Wallace, a 13th century Scottish warrior who led the Scots in the First War of Scottish Independence against King Edward I of England (known as Longshanks). The film was nominated for ten Academy Awards and won five.

This movie is an intense true story with brutal medieval battle scenes. The movie is rated-R, and in our house R movies are not allowed for the youngins. This is the first R-rated movie they get to see with their Dad. It is a great bonding event and a lot of fun.

The story of the movie is how William Wallace becomes motivated to lead the Scots in a war against England. Young William Wallace witnesses the treachery King Edward "Longshanks" against the Scots. Longshanks grants his noblemen land and privileges in Scotland. This included Prima

Nocha. Prima Nocha was the right and privilege of English nobles to sleep with a woman on the first night of her marriage.

William Wallace secretly marries his love to avoid the possiblity of this humiliation. In an unfortunte series of events, the English nobles publically execute William Wallaces wife. This is a horrifying and tragic scene but played to perfection to establish the motive. The motivation is for William Wallace (aka Mel Gibson) to avenge the death of the love of his life. This starts the war, for the love of a woman.

There are many interesting aspects to this movie setup. First is the motivation. What is the reason William Wallace decides to take on the English, for the love of a woman? Love of something is a great motivator. The flip side of this motivation is revenge. Revenge for the death of his wife. Both sides of the love and hate coin is captured by the story of William Wallace and his wife.

Another interesting aspect of this part of the story is how well they establish motivation for action. Eveyone watching this scene knows that Mel Gibson is coming to get retribution. The first big fight scene is Wallace (Gibson) leading his clan to destroy the English garrison.

All throughout the movie, we are reminded of William Wallace's motivation to defend the honor of his slain wife. This makes me think about what motivates us to take action. In some cases, like William Wallace, it is a tragic event. What motivates you?

As the movie proceeds, another motivation is added, and this part of the movie I had forgotten. William Wallace was motivated by **the desire for freedom**. The death of his wife gets him off the couch and moving, but the desire for freedom keeps him motivated. He is motivated by freedom for himself and his countrymen.

Here are some quotes from the movie.

> **William Wallace:** "It's all for nothing if you don't have freedom."
> **William Wallace:** "They may take away our lives, but they'll never take our freedom!"

Royal Magistrate *(who is torturing William Wallace and wants him to pledge allegiance to the king)*:
"The prisoner wishes to say a word."
William Wallace [shouts loud and long]: "Freedom!"

Malcolm Wallace: Your heart is free...have the courage to follow it.

William Wallace: Fight and you may die. Run, and you'll live... at least a while. And dying in your beds, many years from now, would you be willin' to trade ALL the days, from this day to that, for one chance, just one chance, to come back here and tell our enemies that they may take our lives, but they'll never take... OUR FREEDOM!

I watch this movie with my boys because there are so many great lessons in this story. William Wallace was willing to fight and die for freedom. **What are you willing to do for your freedom?**

The desire for freedom is fundamental to the human experience. As far back as you can go, there are stories of humans seeking freedom. The book of Genesis and Exodus in the Bible describe the time of slavery for the Jews in Egypt. It is an epic tale of miraculous deliverance from slavery to the Egyptian Pharaoh.

If you have ever been a slave or felt like a slave, freedom is a great motivator. In modern times we have many freedoms but there are some areas where we are still slaves. You might not consider this, and you may have decided that freedom is really not worth the struggle, but there are more freedoms to be won if you are willing to fight for them.

The most common type of bondage in our culture is debt. The constraints of debt create a type of slavery. As we have discussed, elimination of debt is an important part of your financial plan. **What are you willing to do to be free of debt?**

Financial freedom is what this book is about. It is my desire to motivate and outline a plan of action to help you gain this freedom. **What are you willing to do to create a financial plan? What are you willing to do to be financially free?**

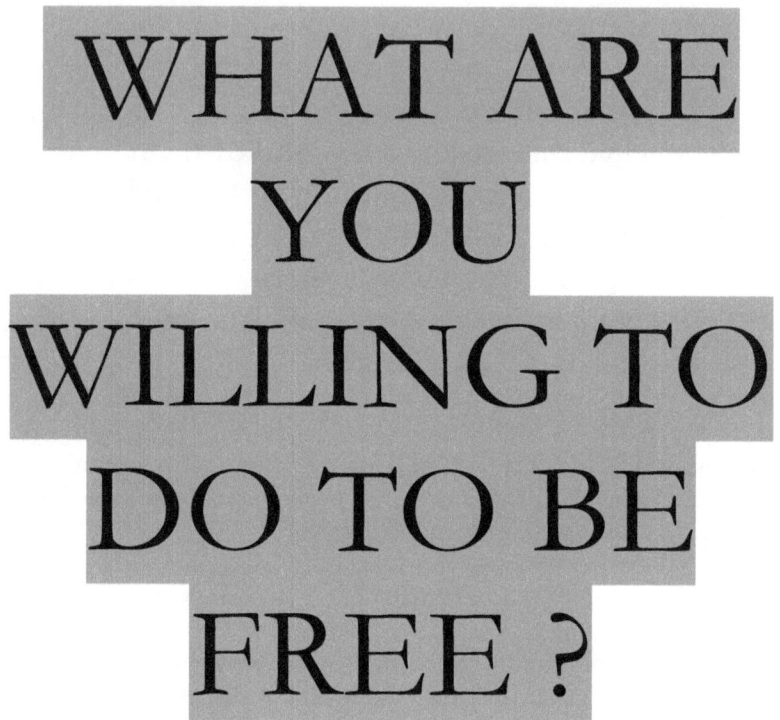

WHAT ARE YOU WILLING TO DO TO BE FREE ?

A modern figure that I think of when I think of freedom is Nelson Mandela. **Nelson Mandela** was imprisoned for 27 years because he was found guilty of conspiracy and sabotage to overthrow the government of South Africa. He was sentenced to life imprisonment in 1964 and was released in 1990 after serving for 27 years in jail. What is remarkable about his story is his attitude of hope and faith that sustained him while in prison. He has become a symbol of perseverance in the face of long odds.

"There is no easy walk to freedom anywhere, and many of us will have to pass through the valley of the shadow of death again and again before we reach the mountaintop of our desires" – **Nelson Mandela**

"For to be free is not merely to cast off one's chains, but to live in a way that respects and enhances the freedom of others." – **Nelson Mandela**

"Hope is a powerful weapon, and (one) no one power on earth can deprive you of." – **Nelson Mandela**

In the first quote, Nelson Mandela is referring to Psalms 23, "*Yea, though* *I walk through the valley of the shadow* **of death, I will fear no evil: for thou art with me; thy rod and thy staff they comfort me."** You may think this is dramatic, but this is the same type of struggle you will face to achieve your financial freedom. It is not easy and the path is not straight, there will be many turns and uncertainties that will change your plan.

The parallel between physical bondage or slavery, and the mental and emotional struggle of financial bondage, is the perfect analogy of the difficulties you will face. Physical slavery like that of Nelson Mandela and the children of Israel experienced it hard. But the mental and emotional slavery of financial bondage can be just as hard.

The focus of these stories of freedom is great to review but there is something missing. There are not many stories written about the slaves that could have sought freedom but gave up and did not try. Stories are not written about these people but their story must be told.

What if you knew freedom was possible but you did not try? When the full history of the world is told, you know there are stories of slaves that could have been free but did not try. Stories of people who heard a story or read a book that outlined the plan for freedom but they did not try. Why not, why did they not try? That goes in the category of "mysteries of the world".

I hope you are starting to see yourself. You have read this far in the book and you are being shown a path to financial freedom.

Are you going to take action and seek your freedom?

When the full story is told, will it come out that you had a chance for freedom and did not try? When you think of the freedom you seek, are you willing to fight the fight and persevere until you see your freedom?

What is True Freedom?

According to Dan Sullivan, the true freedom is freedom of purpose. Dan Sullivan is a management consultant who has worked with entrepreneurs for the last 40 years. He has captured some of the ideas we have been discussing in this book but his focus is on business owners. My focus has been on you, the individual planning for future freedom.

It is his claim that successful people do what they do, not just for the money, but for the higher purpose. And when the money is sufficient to supply all their needs and more, they continue to work on projects that have an impact on their fellow human beings.

This is very interesting for all of us who may be seeking retirement and financial freedom. Do you plan to quit when you achieve your goal and are free? I hope not. When you become financially free is when all the fun begins, if you plan and prepare for it.

Freedom of Time
Freedom of Money
Freedom of Relationship

Freedom of Purpose (the biggest freedom)

All three add up to freedom of purpose. Unfortunately, in our society, the successful have come under attack. The critics say they do what they do only for the money, they say, "they don't care about people". The real story is that successful people are striving to lead the best possible life. Success is a result of this striving. Successful people want to make the biggest positive contribution. For many, they have found a purpose bigger than themselves.

A purpose is the reason why something is done, or created, or exists. Why are you seeking retirement? Why are you seeking financial freedom? Why are you doing all this? Why were you created?

One of the great books about purpose is **The Purpose Driven Life** by Rick Warren. Since it was published in 2002, it has sold over 30 million copies and was on the New York Times Bestseller List for over 90 weeks. I highly recommend this book if you are struggling to get motivated to seek your freedom.

Another newer book about purpose and how to become more inspired at work is **Start with Why: How Great Leaders Inspire Everyone to Take Action**. This book is written for business people who are building business and creating products. I see it as a way to get motivated to take action on your financial plan. I think it could be titled,

START WITH WHY: HOW GREAT PEOPLE INSPIRE THEMSELVES TO TAKE ACTION.

In the book, the author Simon Sinek talks about a golden circle. The outer circle is "how" to do something. In this book we have talked a lot about how to create a financial plan. The next circle inside the outer circle is "what" to do. We have talked a lot about what to do. But the bull's eye and the area of real motivation is WHY. Why create a plan, why try? This is the critical question to resolve.

The ability to motivate yourself is not difficult. It is usually tied to some internal or external factor. For those who are inspired, the motivation to act is deeply personal. Finding that internal or external trigger will get you moving. An internal trigger might be the desire to provide for your family. For William Wallace, the internal trigger was revenge for the death of his wife.

External triggers are well known: the big house, the nice car, the trip around the world. If this motivates you, get a picture of what you seek and put it on your wall. Do whatever it takes to get moving on your financial plan.

When Your WHY is Big Enough... The HOW is Easy!

If you start with why, and determine your purpose, you will have motivation to seek the other freedoms of time, money and relationship. I contend that when you get purpose right, it will drive all the others.

If you are still struggling to find the motivation to start your financial plan, call me, I'd love to talk with you. It is part of my purpose to help you get moving. Let me help you create a financial plan. It is easier to get started than you think.

As my wife loves to tell me, "Marshall, it's all about relationships".

"You will be the same person in five years as you are today except for the people you meet and the books you read."

— Charlie "Tremendous" Jones

"From errors of others,
a wise man corrects his own." -Syrus

Build a Team

This is the truth, you will do better if you find a good coach to help you. If you join a gym, finding a trainer will help you make progress faster than on your own. If you play professional sports, you will have many coaches.

There are superbly qualified, caring and committed financial professionals out there for you. The value of a coach and advisor to you will greatly exceed the cost of the advice. Remember, the advice may provide incrementally better returns AND help you avoid common mistakes AND save you time AND worry. Consider the full costs.

Yes, this is a do-it-yourself society. Home Depot has made billions on this premise. "It's ok if I mow my own lawn, paint my own house, or change my own spark plugs", you reason. "I've got the time, I can save a few dollars, I need the challenge, and besides, I kind of enjoy the excitement of gambling".

On the other hand, I do not want to do surgery on my own heart. I do not want to draw up my own estate plan ... too risky. The cost is money well spent. You live another day because your heart is repaired properly. Your heirs can still talk to one another after you're gone because there's no reason to fight. And who really has the time and temperament to do their own investing?

You might feel this way if you were not constantly bombarded with the do-it-yourself mentality. Just visit the local magazine rack and see all the ways to succeed on your own as an investor. Why pay an advisor to pick mutual funds for me, when I can pick no-load, five-star funds myself?

This line of reasoning sounds seductively logical until you examine the unspoken premise. The premise is the wealth comes from individual fund selection. This is NOT true. **Wealth is not determined by investment performance, wealth is determined by investor behavior.** Think about that for a minute. The wealth of the greatest investors in the world is the result of, first and foremost, their behavior. This has been proven by research. The critical issue is what you do, and avoid doing.

This is common sense that is not all that common. If you think about it for a minute you will realize that to get exceptional performance you have to act in a way that will allow that performance to occur.

This is easier said than done. And that is why we are talking about it. Behavior precedes performance. And if you get scared and sell at the wrong time, your investment performance will suffer. If you forget your principles in the heat of the battle, your performance will suffer.

This is a big issue. Emotions and perceptions determine how well you will do in life. And that is why you need a knowledgeable and caring team. We all need help to face some of the big issues that we all face as investors.

Can you achieve the optimal health you want by using only the advice in a $20 dollar diet-and-exercise book? Possibly. Consider how you've done with diet and exercise in the past. You may have a gift for diet-and-exercise. Most of us don't. The only question is: what does the help cost and what is it worth to you?

These days, a professional investment advisor costs around 1% a year. This one-percent is based on the size of your investment portfolio. You may get a break based on the size of your portfolio but this is a good starting point.

And so, the question to ask yourself is … Will working with an advisor add more than 1% to your total lifetime return? Does it seem likely to you that an advisor's counsel will increase your return by more than 1% a year? Does it seem possibly that a qualified advisor may save you more than 1% a year in mistakes you do not make? Can an advisor save you time, effort and worry? If you believe the answer is yes to any one of these questions, you need to get busy and find a high-quality advisor today.

If you believe the answer is NO. Skip to the end of this book and use what you have learned. Good luck.

If you're still reading, it means you remain willing to entertain the idea of listening. And you are willing to look for an advisor. The question then becomes: exactly what kind of help do you need?

Think of all the aspects of your financial life: wills, trusts, mortgages, insurance, budgeting, and on and on. These are financial planning issues. The person you need to help you is a financial planner. If you have these issues taken care of and you want someone who just works on investing, you need an investment advisor.

Now all you need to do is find an advisor that is right for you. Advisors today are better trained, better supervised and more highly regulated (if you think that's a good thing) than ever before. They are subjected to rigorous training. They command an awesome array of software and technology. This enables them to create sophisticated planning scenarios and intensive investment comparisons.

If you think you can find equivalent tools for free on the Internet, think again. They ain't there.

The really good advisors are energized and enthusiastic about their ability to help clients and ensure they live well in their later years. This is a high calling and one that the great advisors do not take lightly. If you've ever counseled anyone who has made poor financial decisions, you would understand the value of top-quality financial advice.

If you are clear on what you want to accomplish it will be easier to find the right advisor for you. If you understand the difference between a planning issue and an investment issue, you will be able to choose the correct type of person.

Beware of the "I can do all things for all people" advisor. This is all too common. And for someone who does not understand the landscape of the financial world it can be truly confusing. Here are a few simple ideas to consider. If someone's primary label and brand is … insurance. Most likely, their expertise will be insurance. Insurance products have some element of investments but in most cases they are insurance products. It's important to be able to distinguish the difference. If their brand is related to real estate and mortgages, this is where their expertise most likely lies.

To find the right advisor can be difficult. Here are a few thoughts to consider in your search.

First, the advisor who is right for you listens to you and cares about you. Mutual respect, empathy, and a shared sense of values are the critical elements in a successful advisor/client relationship. Without these values, it will not work well. You should be able to feel the advisor's genuine interest in you. You should be able to feel his desire to do good for you and your family.

You should never feel pressured to do anything. You are engaging in a lifelong quest for wealth. This may affect your family for generations. The idea that something has to be invested today or you'll miss it may not be in the best interest of the client. This is not to say that your advisor should not encourage you to be decisive and act promptly. And over time, a good advisor will understand your tendencies. If you are a procrastinator, a good advisor will push you to make a decision.

The right advisor for you makes you feel comfortable. This should be like talking to your family doctor. This relationship works both ways. You have to be willing to answer the advisor's questions, just as you would with a doctor. If she says, "Where does it hurt?" you can't say, "I can't tell you that". A good advisor will not fall for this. A good advisor, like a good doctor, needs to understand the situation before they can prescribe a medication or solution.

While it is important to have an advisor whose technical capabilities you respect, it will be far more important to have an advisor that you trust. Remember, this is someone you will trust with your family's financial life. Are you willing to allow them to do surgery on your finances? As the old saying goes … "it's not important how much they know, it's important that you know they care".

To find a financial advisor, start with friends, family and neighbors. And start with the friends, family and neighbors that seem to be doing well financially. (good point) You might ask the senior management at the company you work for to provide a name of an advisor. A recommendation from someone who is benefiting from an advisor's counsel is a good place to start. Also, your attorney or accountant will probably have found advisors they respect and can refer you to them.

If your own circle of acquaintances fails to help you find someone you like, you can obtain a list of financial planners from the Financial Planning Association (FPA). Visit www.fpanet.org.

An organization of financial planners who work on a fee-only basis can be found at the National Association of Personal Financial Advisors. (NAPFA). A fee-only advisor does not receive any commission for the investments they recommend.) Visit them at www.napfa.org.

Although it will be time consuming, this is an important first step in improving your future. Remember, this is a learning process and may be confusing at first. Persevere and you will be the better for it. And when you build a team, you will start to see the value they provide.

All successful progress, first and foremost, is act of faith in the future. There is no better place to start than choosing a team and placing your trust in them.

Conversely, there is no worse start then concluding ... "you can't trust any of them". Deciding to do it yourself for economic reasons is one thing but electing to do it yourself because advisors, as a group, can't be trusted is a symptom of other emotional problems. Tough talk I know, but this is an important issue.

It is no harder to find a good support team than it is to find a good doctor, lawyer or accountant. Good and trustworthy people are available to work for you, if you are willing to look. You just need to be willing to look and ask.

Just remember, the value of a good team is a worth more than it costs. That's all that matters. Make the calls. Good luck in your search.

Be Prepared, Be Prepared...

We have come to the end of the book and my message to you is "be prepared, be prepared". This phrase is funny to me because it is a song in the animated movie, **Hoodwinked**. This is a very good movie that I have watched many times with my kids. I'm not sure why this song is in the movie but it is a good motivator to do some financial planning. (If you want to hear the song, search youtube.com for "hoodwinked be prepared song").

The lyrics capture it perfectly.

**Be prepared, be prepared,
This lesson must be shared,
This lesson must be shared,
Be prepared!**

**Be prepared, be prepared
And unless you got a spare,
You got one life, so handle it with care
So, be prepared!
(Goat yodeling)**

The message is fantastic and the goat yodeling is even better.

This book started by suggesting that your chances of financial success will improve if you prepare. My purpose in writing this book has been to help you think and act in a way that increases your wealth and provides a retirement plan that serves and protects you and your family.

Freedom is a great motivator and something I've been seeking for many years now. My life started in Tennessee in 1963 but my desire for growth and education led me to California to attend college. During college I worked at HP Labs in Palo Alto. HP Labs is one of the great corporate research laboratories in the world. They do research in an effort to innovate and lead the company with new products.

Early in life I worked with some of the smartest people in the world. These people had engineering degrees, masters and doctorates from Stanford, MIT & CalTECH (to name a few). What I noticed about them was that they were always learning new things. I can remember being amazed at all the things they knew (and I had the opportunity to have lunch with them **every day** and ask questions). This experience instilled in me a deep desire to be continually learning new things.

Becoming a life-long learner has allowed me to grow and change and create the life that I desire. If we seek, we will find. I did not make that up, that is found in the ancient text of the Bible. In my life, I have been seeking to learn and build something of value. Although, it has not turned out exactly like I imagined, it has turned out to be even better.

Throughout my journey, I have been seeking freedom all along. I have been seeking freedom of association. I am truly free to associate with those people I enjoy being around. There were times in my life when "I had to" attend a meeting I did not want to attend. That is not my story any longer.

I am free to work with people that I enjoy being around. There was a time in my corporate life that I ended up working for one of the worst people in the world. (name withheld for legal reasons ;) This person had the worst character of anyone I have ever experienced in my life. This was a great strain on me. Going to work each day was not fun. The experience was very painful. In retrospect, it was a blessing because it motivated me to make an important change.

My story now is that if I encounter someone who is not enjoyable to be around, I have the power to choose to not associate with them again. This is a wonderful freedom. It adds happiness to my life to know I have this power. My goal is to work with clients that I can help and that will listen to my advice and whom I enjoy being around. This makes for a wonderful life, believe me.

I am free to work on projects that I enjoy. Many times, we are not free to choose where we will dedicate our time and effort. This is a freedom I have achieved. The projects I work on provide benefit and serve my many clients and friends. This makes me happy.

When I show up each day, I have the opportunity to help people navigate the complex world of money and finances. This is exciting. It is risky, and it is rewarding. For me, it is a great reward to have the opportunity to serve my clients, family and friends.

My plan is to find work that I enjoy and keep doing it until the day I die. Having a financial plan is a part of this master plan. Helping you create a financial plan is also a part of this master plan. And, it is something I can do for the next 50 years. Who knows! You don't know, I don't know. But, I do have a plan.

My path to freedom is different than yours but it has been my desire to encourage and help you along your path. You may be further along the path than I am, I may be further along the path than you, but I am still seeking new horizons. One of the amazing blessings of this life is that there are always new horizons to seek.

May the road rise up to meet you.
May the wind be always at your back.
May the sun shine warm upon your face;
the rains fall soft upon your fields
and until we meet again,
may God hold you in the palm of His hand.

You can contact Marshall at …
marshall@clarionadvisors.com

1519 Lincoln Way
Auburn CA 95603
(800) 748-6575

Appendix A:
IRS Contribution Limits for 2017

401(k)s. The annual contribution limit for employees who participate in 401(k), 403(b), most 457 plans, and the federal government's Thrift Savings Plan, is $18,000 for 2017, the same as in 2016. Note, you can make changes to your 401(k) election at any time during the year, not just during open enrollment season when most employers send you a reminder to update your elections for the next plan year.

The 401(k) Catch-Up. The catch-up contribution limit for employees age 50 or older in these plans also stays the same at $6,000 for 2017. Even if you don't turn 50 until Dec. 31, 2017, you can make the additional $6,000 catch-up contribution for the year.

SEP IRAs and Solo 401(k)s. For the self-employed and small business owners, the amount they can save in a SEP IRA or a solo 401(k) is up from $53,000 in 2016 to $54,000 in 2017. That's based on the amount they can contribute as an employer, as a percentage of their salary; the compensation limit used in the savings calculation also goes up from $265,000 in 2016 to $270,000 in 2017.

After-tax 401(k) contributions. If your employer allows after-tax contributions to your 401(k), you also get the advantage of the $54,000 limit for 2017. It's an overall cap, including your $18,000 (pre-tax or Roth) salary deferrals plus any employer contributions (but not catch-up contributions).

The SIMPLE. The limit on SIMPLE retirement accounts for 2017 is $12,500, the same as in 2016. The SIMPLE catch-up limit is still $3,000.

Defined Benefit Plans. The limitation on the annual benefit of a defined benefit plan goes up from $210,000 in 2016 to $215,000 in 2017. These are powerful pension plans (an individual version of the kind that used to be more common in the corporate world before 401(k)s took over) for high-earning self-employed folks.

Individual Retirement Accounts. The $5,500 limit on annual contributions to an Individual Retirement Account remains the same for 2017, the fifth year in a row. The catch-up contribution limit, which is not subject to inflation adjustments, remains at $1,000. (Remember that 2016 IRA contributions can be made until April 15th, 2017.)

Deductible IRA phase-outs. You can earn a little more in 2017 and get to deduct your contributions to a traditional pre-tax IRA. Note, even if you earn too much to get a deduction for contributing to an IRA, you can still contribute; it's just non-deductible.

In 2017, the deduction for taxpayers making contributions to a traditional IRA is phased out for singles and heads of household who are covered by a workplace retirement plan and have modified adjusted gross incomes (AGI) between $62,000 and $72,000, up from $61,000 and $71,000 in 2016. For married couples filing jointly, in which the spouse who makes the IRA contribution is covered by a workplace retirement plan, the income phase-out range is $99,000 to $119,000, up from $98,000 to $118,000.

For an IRA contributor who is not covered by a workplace retirement plan and is married to someone who is covered, the deduction is phased out if the couple's income is between $186,000 and $196,000 in 2017, up from $184,000 and $194,000 in 2016. For a married individual filing a separate return who is covered by a workplace retirement plan, the phase-out range is not subject to an annual cost-of-living adjustment and remains $0 to $10,000.

Roth IRA Phase-Outs. The same adjustment helps Roth IRA savers. In 2017, the AGI phase-out range for taxpayers making contributions to a Roth IRA is $186,000 to $196,000 for married couples filing jointly, up from $184,000 to $194,000 in 2016. For singles and heads of household, the income phase-out range is $118,000 to $133,000, up from $117,000 to $132,000 in 2015.

If you earn too much to open a Roth IRA, you can open a nondeductible IRA and convert it to a Roth IRA as Congress lifted any income restrictions for Roth IRA conversions.

Bibliography

1. PREFACE
   1.1. Pilon, Marc. "Most Americans Haven't Planned for Retirement and Other Areas of Concern". < http://blogs.wsj.com/economics/2011/06/06/most-americans-havent-planned-for-retirement-and-other-areas-of-concern/?KEYWORDS=Lusardi >. June 6, 2011.
   1.2. Sinek, Simon. "How Great Leaders Inspire Action". < https://www.ted.com/talks/simon_sinek_how_great_leaders_inspire_action >. September 2009.
2. Introduction
   2.1. Katie, Byron. "Work and Money". Byron Katie International. 2006.
   2.2. Rohn, Jim. "The Art of Exceptional Living". Simon & Shuster. March 1, 2003.
   2.3. Adams, Scott. "How to Fail at Almost Everything and Still Win Big". Portfolio. 2013.
3. Part 1 – The Preparation
   3.1. Rath, Tom. "Strengthfinder 2.0". Gallup Press. 2007.
   3.2. Bolles, Richard N. "What Color Is Your Parachute". Ten Speed Press. 2016.
   3.3. Ramsey, Dave. "The Total Money Makeover". Thomas Nelson. 2008.
4. Part 2: The Plan
   4.1. Investment Plan
      4.1.1. Malkiel, Burton. "A Random Walk Down Wall Street". W.W. Norton & Company. 1973.
      4.1.2. WSJ. "The Dying Business of Picking Stocks". <google>. October 17, 2016.
      4.1.3. Arnold, Chris. "Yale Money Whiz Shares Tips on Growing a Nest Egg". < http://www.npr.org/templates/story/story.php?storyId=89324244>. April 3, 2008.
      4.1.4. Fabrikant, Geraldine. "Yale Endowment Earned 3.4% in a Year When Many Peers Lost". < http://www.nytimes.com/2016/09/24/business/yale-university-endowment.html?_r=0>. Sept 23, 2016.
      4.1.5. Robbins, Tony. "The End of the Bull Market". < https://www.tonyrobbins.com/wealth-lifestyle/the-end-of-the-bull-market/>. July 2016.
      4.1.6. Wikipedia. "List of Stock Market Indices". < https://en.wikipedia.org/wiki/List_of_stock_market_indices>. December 2016.

4.1.7. Lambert, Craig. "The Marketplace of Perceptions". <http://harvardmagazine.com/2006/03/the-marketplace-of-perce.html>. March 2006.

4.2. Income Plan

    4.2.1. Updegrave, Walter. "A Three-Step Plan to Getting the Retirement Income You Need". < http://money.cnn.com/2015/08/13/retirement/retirement-income-plan />. August 2015.

4.3. Insurance Planning

    4.3.1. Pareta, Cathy. "Investopia: Intro to Insurance". <http://www.investopedia.com/university/insurance/insurance1.asp>. December 2016.

    4.3.2. Williams, Geoff. "3 types of insurance you need, and 3 you don't". < http://money.usnews.com/money/personal-finance/articles/2014/09/02/3-types-of-insurance-you-need-and-3-you-dont>. Sept 2, 2014

    4.3.3. Life Happens. "Permanent Insurance". <http://www.lifehappens.org/insurance-overview/permanent-insurance/>. December 2016.

4.4. Tax Planning

    4.4.1. Russell, Jason. "Look at how many pages are in the federal tax code". < http://www.washingtonexaminer.com/look-at-how-many-pages-are-in-the-federal-tax-code/article/2563032>. April 15, 2016.

    4.4.2. Hodge, Scott. "Putting a Face on America's Tax Returns". < http://taxfoundation.org/slideshow/putting-face-americas-tax-returns>. Oct 21, 2013.

    4.4.3. Bischoff, Bill. "Why tax planning is so important". < http://www.marketwatch.com/story/why-tax-planning-is-so-important-2014-07-01>. July 1, 2014.

    4.4.4. Anspach, Dana. "What is a Tax-Deferred Investment Account". < https://www.thebalance.com/tax-deferred-savings-account-and-investments-2388988 >. Oct 16, 2016.

    4.4.5. Farrington, Sam. "7 Advantages of Investing in Taxable Accounts". < https://www.nerdwallet.com/blog/investing/7-advantages-of-investing-in-taxable-accounts/>. Feb 19, 2016.

    4.4.6. CNN Money. "Ultimate guide to retirement". < http://money.cnn.com/retirement/guide/investing_taxes.moneymag/index8.htm>. Dec 2016.

4.4.7. Slott, Ed. "2016 Retirement Decisions Guide". IRAHelp LLC. 2016.

4.4.8. Slott, Ed. "Retirement Savings Time Bomb". PenguinBooks. 2012.

4.5. Estate Planning

4.5.1. CNN Money. "Ultimate Guide to Retirement Planning: What is estate planning?". <http://money.cnn.com/retirement/guide/estateplanning_basics.moneymag/>. Dec 2016.

4.5.2. Estateplanning.com. "What is Estate Planning". <http://www.estateplanning.com/What-is-Estate-Planning/>. Dec 2016.

4.5.3. The Learnvest Staff. "Estate Planning: Your Need-To-Know". <http://www.forbes.com/sites/learnvest/2013/05/24/estate-planning-your-need-to-know/#4e6b54c7694b>. May 24, 2013.

4.5.4. Fidelity Viewpoints. "Do you need an estate plan". <https://www.fidelity.com/viewpoints/personal-finance/do-you-need-an-estate-plan>. Jan 10, 2017.

5. Part 3: The Freedom

5.1. Wikipedia. "Braveheart". < https://en.wikipedia.org/wiki/Braveheart>. December 2016.

5.2. Wikipedia. "Jews in Egypt". < https://en.wikipedia.org/wiki/History_of_the_Jews_in_Egypt>. December 2016.

5.3. Wikipedia. "Nelson Mandela". < https://en.wikipedia.org/wiki/Nelson_Mandela>. December 2016.

5.4. Sullivan, Dan. "Freedom of Purpose". <http://now.strategiccoach.com/Freedom_of_Purpose_Nurture>. December 2016.

5.5. Sinek, Simon. "A summary of the book: Start with Why" < http://www.pearsonandassociates.co.uk/uploads/files/start-with-why-by-simon-sinek.pdf>. Dec 2016.

5.6. Gaither, Benjy. "Lyrics: Be Prepared". < http://www.songonlyrics.net/soundtracks/hoodwinked2009-be-prepared-lyrics.html>. Dec 2016.

6. Appendix A

6.1. Ebeling, Ashlea. "IRS Announces 2017 Retirement Plan Contribution Limits". http://www.forbes.com/sites/ashleaebeling/2016/10/27/irs-announces-2017-retirement-plans-contributions-limits-for-401ks-and-more/#371f203056e20. Oct 23, 2016.

About the Author

Marshall Goins was born in Gallatin Tennessee near Nashville in 1963, and began his career as an investment professional in 2003.

He is a husband, father of four boys and musician. Marshall has been an investor, manager, student and business owner since 1982.

Before becoming an investment advisor, Marshall worked as a corporate manager for Hewlett-Packard, Digital Impact, and Safeway.